THE ALLEY *of* LOVE
and YELLOW JASMINES

THE ALLEY *of* LOVE
and YELLOW JASMINES

A MEMOIR

Shohreh Aghdashloo

HARPER
www.harpercollins.com

The names and identifying characteristics of some of the individuals featured throughout this book have been changed to protect their privacy.

THE ALLEY OF LOVE AND YELLOW JASMINES. Copyright © 2013 by Shohreh Aghdashloo. All rights reserved. Printed in the United States of America. No part of this book may be used or reproduced in any manner whatsoever without written permission except in the case of brief quotations embodied in critical articles and reviews. For information, address Harper-Collins Publishers, 10 East 53rd Street, New York, NY 10022.

HarperCollins books may be purchased for educational, business, or sales promotional use. For information, please e-mail the Special Markets Department at SPsales@harpercollins.com.

All photographs are courtesy of the author unless otherwise noted.

FIRST EDITION

Designed by Jo Anne Metsch

Library of Congress Cataloging-in-Publication Data has been applied for.

ISBN: 978-0-06-200980-7

13 14 15 16 17   OV/RRD   10 9 8 7 6 5 4 3 2 1

For Tara and Houshang,
my heart and soul,
and for my beloved parents

CONTENTS

THE ALLEY *of* LOVE
and YELLOW JASMINES

1

THE OSCARS

I T IS NOW the eleventh hour. Time is passing quickly. My childhood dream has come true, and I am spellbound. It is the day of the Oscars, February 29, 2004. I have been nominated for Best Actress in a Supporting Role for my portrayal of Nadi Behrani, the submissive, voiceless wife of Colonel Behrani, played by Ben Kingsley in the movie *House of Sand and Fog*, based on the novel by Andre Dubus III.

Only a few days before, the last Queen of Iran, Farah Pahlavi, called me to make a special request that I not wear Valentino for the glorious night as planned but rather a dress by a designer from Iran, my homeland. Simin and her assistant are at my house to help me get into the tight red silk satin gown that she has created for me. They are in my bedroom now, steaming and stitching the last bits and pieces, making sure nothing moves or could fall off during the event. The dress has required the talents of five tailors and forty-eight hours of beading in preparation for this day.

Erin, a freelance makeup artist, has taken over the den of our four-bedroom house, which is located in a pretty, flower-draped gated community in Calabasas about twenty-five miles from Los Angeles. Erin has spread her beautifying tools over the entire surface of my faded and stained vintage blue wooden desk, a reminder of another time, another era.

A gentleman named Mark has come from Harry Winston with the jewelry I will be wearing to complete my fairy-tale evening. The jewels include an exquisite bracelet of rubies and diamonds, with matching earrings, along with a ten-carat diamond ring. Mark is going to stay with me throughout the night to keep a close eye on the million-dollar jewels, so that I won't run away with them back to the Caspian Sea.

Tara-Jane, my fourteen-year-old daughter, is upset that her little black dress has a torn zipper and there is no Plan B. She wants to go to the Oscars in casual clothing. Houshang, my husband—also an actor, as well as a director and playwright—looks dashing in his black Valentino tuxedo and is doing his best to convince our daughter that the Oscars is all about one's achievement and the celebration of one's art.

"So be it!" he says eventually, with his unique respect for his creative offspring. "Put on a T-shirt and a pair of jeans and enjoy the night!"

Seeing that she has properly won this test of wills, Tara hurries to her room to change. I am glad she is a young woman who makes her own choices and has the right to do so. Yes, it would have been nice to see her all dressed up, but she is always lovely to me. She is the joy of my life.

Mahwah, my girlfriend, also from my homeland, is suffering from advanced lung cancer, but she has requested to be with me while I am getting ready for the biggest night of my life. I am glad to have her there, though we barely get a chance to talk. We just smile at each other each time I pass through the living room, where she is resting on a sofa and watching me. She is so happy for me, and I am pleased to see her smile.

Other people who have gathered at my house include my longtime friend Jaleh (whose nickname is Zsa Zsa, but not because of the Gabors. Having nicknames was customary back in my time in Iran.) and Mansur Sepehrband, a prominent Iranian talk show host. He is here to capture all of the intimate details of the Hollywood ritual with his high-tech digital camera. It will air this afternoon before the Oscars on Jam-e-Jam TV, a Farsi-speaking satellite network that broadcasts around the world, including my birth country. I am the first Iranian and Middle Eastern actor to be nominated for an Academy Award. Sometimes I feel the weight of the world on my shoulders for the people of my former country. Millions of their hearts will be with me tonight. I particularly think of the many women who have been silenced in my homeland by the dictatorship. They will be secretly cheering me on.

Somewhere in the midst of all of this, for the briefest of moments, I am having an out-of-body experience, observing myself in this holographic scene. I am calm and happy, but the so-called butterflies in my stomach are at unrest. I am talking, moving, sitting, and standing, but my soul is flying through the universe fast, seeking the sun, longing for a moment in its pure light. My soul is whirling, celebrating a dream coming true in this land of dream-makers—the land of freedom and democracy.

At last it is 3:00 P.M., and DreamWorks, the production studio of *House of Sand and Fog*, has sent a shiny black stretch limo to take us to the Oscars, which are being held at the Kodak Theatre in Hollywood. We are ready to leave for what turns out to be an hour-and-a-half drive in traffic. I have to lie down on the backseat, as forcefully suggested by the designer, so that my dress will remain perfect. It is a vast understatement to say that I'm feeling uncomfortable. All I hear is Simin echoing, "All actors do the same thing to avoid wrinkles on their dress. You will thank me when you see the pictures."

Mansur holds his camera next to the window and asks his final question before Jaleh, Houshang, Tara-Jane, Mark, and I drive away:

"Shohreh, do you think you are going to win?" I have not seriously contemplated this question. The Academy has not seen my body of work yet. That remains in Iran. *House of Sand and Fog* is my debut to people in Hollywood and America at large. I simply choose not to answer his question.

I have had the pleasure to work with one of my favorite actors of all time, Sir Ben Kingsley. It had been a dream of mine that finally came true. When I was in my early twenties, I sat mesmerized as I watched him perform in a play in London. Teary-eyed, I told my mother that I would only call myself a real actress when I had worked with Kingsley.

Any serenity I was holding on to melts away as we arrive at the theater and in the endless line of stretch limousines. There is no amount of preparation for the experience of being on the red carpet. The photographers' flashes of quick lights are pale in comparison to the number of movie stars present.

Actors and actresses walk the red carpet—almost a block long—to the Kodak Theatre. They are surrounded by fans on the right, seemingly pouring off of the scaffolding, and a sea of prominent media personalities on the left. Underneath the warm early twilight, I feel proud of having followed my dream and not given up every time my life turned upside down.

I HAVE TO constantly remind myself that this is not a dream. The reporters are kind to me. They often say that I am the "dark horse," or the surprise of this year's Oscars. Even Joan Rivers is respectful, except for one faux pas—which I know she doesn't mean to make—introducing me as Shohreh "Ashashasloo," which in Farsi means "contaminated with urine."

The red-carpet journey ends much too quickly. In what seems like the blink of an eye, an usher escorts us to our seats in the first row. I am right next to Nicole Kidman and her friend. I am so thrilled to be this close to her. I do not feel the same enthusiasm in return.

Next to Nicole's friend is my fellow nominee Renée Zellweger, wearing a whitish gown with a huge matching bow on the back, which takes up so much of her chair she is forced to sit on its edge. She is speaking with a man I assume is her agent, who tries to reassure her, as do Nicole and her friend. I am pleasantly surprised to see that she is nervous, but I think I am less so because I'm new to Hollywood and Renée is a veteran. *Cold Mountain* is her latest movie.

As a fellow actor but also as a fan, I would love to talk to Nicole. But I am completely at a loss for words. She is a megastar. My hope is that she will turn her head to the right and see me and we would instantly burst into conversation about our work, and Hollywood. But it is clear that she is here to support Renée and has no intention of acknowledging me. I understand.

Nevertheless, we do lock eyes for a moment when she turns around to look at my daughter, who is kissing my forehead and wishing me the best. But she turns away before I get a chance to say hello.

Farther down in the first row are Michael Douglas and his gorgeous wife, Catherine Zeta-Jones, standing from her chair. She repeatedly gestures toward Renée with a thumbs-up. She mouths silently, saying, "Renée you are going to win." She does this a few times to make sure Renée receives the message. Finally the curtain goes up and the show begins with Billy Crystal, who sings the entire list of nominees' names in his opening skit. All too soon, the best-supporting-actress nominees' names are called out. My heart is pounding, my thoughts on the ride that brought me to the Oscars. It has certainly been a long one.

"And the award goes to . . ."

2

THE SWEETNESS OF YOUTH

M Y PARENTS LOVED each other to death, for they had both tasted the bitterness of separation. My mother, Effie, was a seemingly great candidate for matchmakers. Elderly female members of the family took pleasure in finding the right match for their granddaughters. But Effie wanted to become a teacher before marrying and continued studying to get her diploma. She was in her sophomore year when she met my father, Anushiravan (named after a righteous nontyrannical Persian king) Vaziritabar. She was studying at the house of her best friend and classmate, my aunt Shamsi. My father, Shamsi's brother, joined them for a brief moment, and it was love at first sight for both of them.

Although he was talking to Shamsi, my father could not take his eyes off my mother, with her beautiful ivory skin, arched eyebrows, shiny brown hair, and light hazel eyes. My father was a quiet, dignified, and handsome young man with gentle manners and an incredible resemblance to the actor David Niven.

Their love was too strong for them to wait for her diploma, so my father asked for my mother's hand. Unfortunately, he was offended when my mother's father demanded a large wedding and a form of financial agreement to compensate for my mother's dowry, in case of a divorce. (This situation, which is typical in Iran, is called *mehre*.)

My mother could not believe it. She was too proud to say anything, or to go back to Shamsi's house and talk to her brother. She was forlorn and over time lost a great deal of weight. My mother kept busy reading romantic novels and immersed herself in other people's love stories.

But not even *Madame Bovary* and the character's unconventional life could help my mother stop thinking about my father. Whenever the doorbell rang, her heart beat more quickly because she thought it might be him, giving in to her father's demands.

A year later, my grandfather Hassan, a military man, decided to put an end to his daughter's misery and dangerous weight loss. He made a surprise visit to my father at the Ministry of Health, where he was employed as an accountant. Hassan placed a fresh red rose from his garden on my father's desk and said, "My daughter is in love with you." Effie and Anushiravan married soon after.

I WAS BORN into a middle-class Iranian family on May 11, 1952, at Fowzia Hospital, in the heart of Tehran. My name, Shohreh, was chosen by my grandfather Jahangir, my father's father. He was partially educated in France and loved poetry. In fact, when my father gave him the news of my birth and asked him if he had a name for me in mind, Grandpa was reading the poetry of Hafez, the fourteenth-century Persian lyric poet who wrote extensively about faith and hypocrisy. He was as well known as Robert Frost, and his works were found in most Iranians' homes. Grandfather randomly chose a page and found my name in the first verse. *Shohreh* means famous. "I am the one who is famous for loving others and being loved."

My newly married mother still loved to go out with her friends and trusted only her mother, Bahar al-Sadat, to take care of me. I began sleeping at Grandmother's quite often before I even knew how to speak. My overnight stays would continue until I was fifteen years old. My grandmother's unconditional love had turned her house into a safe haven for me. She was beautiful and fragile, with curly blond hair, green eyes, and porcelain skin. I loved staying with her and listening to her fascinating stories—even if I didn't yet know what they meant. I loved the sound of her voice.

Once a month, as I grew, we would go to the bazaar to shop, then we would hire a cab to take us to a slum area of Tehran. She politely knocked on half-open doors and respectfully offered her donations: rice, chocolate, dried fruits or even soaps, and whatever else she may have bought that day.

Lavish yet cozy, Grandmother's house was in a row of traditional old houses with multiple courtyards. The outer courtyard led to entry doors with two different doorknobs—one for males and the other for females. The inner courtyard was an unforgettable garden with a variety of flowers such as daisies, tuberoses, and forget-me-nots, sweetbriar, marvel-of-peru, and lush, aromatic red roses. It contained a fishpond with a dozen red goldfish swimming happily under the tepid current. I remember how I would carefully watch them with my hands in the water, anticipating the awkward sensation of touching their tender and slippery flesh. Instead, they would quickly disperse and swim as far away as possible.

Facing the pond was a king-size wooden platform bed covered by Persian rugs. My grandmother, grandfather, and I spent hours lying on it, having dinner, taking a nap, or watching the last reflection of the sun on the emerald green water of the fishpond.

GRANDMOTHER TOOK A nap for exactly one hour every afternoon, between two and three. Therefore, I too had to rest next to her. She would tie my toe to her big toe, using a piece of string. This was her way of making sure that I would not go anywhere unsupervised while she was sleeping—and my way of learning how to remain still, which would later come in handy in my chosen profession.

We dined under the dark turquoise sky, lit by thousands of glittering stars, and listened to the sound of the nightingales throughout the warm summer evenings. We sat cross-legged on the platform and feasted on rice, Persian stew, bread, and yogurt, followed by sweet Persian delights such as baklava and tea. It was usually during tea that my grandfather would tell us stories about whirling dervishes, which could best be described as Persian Buddhists, who desired nothing material but rather

searched for spiritual enlightenment. He spoke of their cere-
monies, in which they experienced religious ecstasy.

My favorite story, which I still tell friends to this day, in-
volves a rich man who leaves his family and lavish estate behind
to become a dervish. The only belongings he takes are a bowl
and the clothes he is wearing. After a couple of hours of walking in the forest, he stops by a river to fill his bowl with water
to drink. When he's finished, he starts walking again on his
endless journey. Another dervish comes upon his bowl and
soon meets up with him to say that he left his bowl behind. The
formerly wealthy man returns to the river then tosses his bowl
high into the sky and far into the river. The other dervish asks
him why he did that, to which the new dervish replies, "Up
until now, no other materials could have stopped me from
looking for the divine. Yet I had to return to get this bowl. As of
this moment, nothing will ever stop me on my path seeking the
truth."

Grandfather believed that true dervishes are revered people,
not only for their spiritual journey in life but also for their courage to strip off their titles and possessions.

Grandmother and I would turn on the radio as soon as
Grandfather went to bed and listen to her favorite program,
One Thousand and One Nights, the saga of Scheherazade. The
sultan of the land has sentenced Scheherazade to death. How-
ever, the clever Scheherazade keeps postponing her death by
telling the sultan a new story every night, which leads to the
following night and the night after that, and so on. Fascinated
and mesmerized by Scheherazade's intriguing tales, I would
put my head on Grandma's lap, and she would stroke my curly

black hair. The radio play ended every night with the narrator announcing, "And when the sultan went to sleep, Scheherazade remained silent until the following night of the one thousand and one nights."

Afterward I would follow Grandmother up the narrow staircase to the flat roof, where we would sleep on our firm mattresses on wooden beds, under a drapery of mosquito nets. Here I would rest flat on my back, gazing at the radiant silver stars through the sheer filter of the net. Anticipating the eleventh stroke of the giant bell of the magnificent Sepah-Salar Mosque around the corner from us, I thought of Scheherazade escaping death, and eventually would fall to sleep.

My grandmother lost her own mother when she gave birth to her third child. Since my grandmother was only two at the time, she could barely remember her mother's face, though she could remember her scent.

"My mother smelled like white jasmine," Grandma used to say. "Did you know she was blond like me? People say she was as beautiful as an *houri* [an angel] and a gracious young woman, too."

Grandmother was raised by her nanny under the supervision of her first stepmother, Khanoom. She was extremely pale with piercing black eyes and soft black hair. She came from a respectable merchant family. Although she was petite, she walked like a tall woman, with her head held high. She was extremely confident, demanding, and very religious till the end of her long life. She passed away at the age of ninety-two.

Grandmother was ten years old when her father, Husain Amir Hamzeh, a wealthy landowner, went to Kerman, in southern Iran, to purchase a piece of land and meet and marry his third wife, Shams, meaning "the sun," a beautiful young woman from a wealthy family as well.

Grandmother always remembered the day she was taken to her second stepmother's house. She was riveted by Shams. Her eyes were sea green and her hair was as black as the winter nights. Shams was tall and slim, and had been married once for a short time but divorced her husband—with her family's consent—as he was thought to be impotent.

She came to Tehran with a couple of large chests bearing her belongings and her dowry, and her personal bondmaid named Fatima. Everybody adored Fatima, and although she had come to us as a part of my great-grandfather's third wife's dowry, she never stopped loving and caring for the whole family.

Fatima was one of the daughters of a self-proclaimed sultan in the Persian Gulf. She was abducted when she was eight years old along with her six-year-old sister while boating in the gulf with their chaperones.

The kidnappers had covered the girls' heads with potato sacks and taken them to a slave market. They sold them to wealthy merchants searching for young and strong domestic help. Fatima had worked for another family for several years before being sold into Shams's family. By this time, she remembered little of the details of her capture. Unfortunately, Fatima's sister was sold to another merchant in another market, and Fatima had no idea of her sister's fate. She believed that their parents must have done everything in their power to find them, but finding them in another country must have been like searching for a needle in a haystack.

TWO YEARS AFTER I was born, my mother gave birth to my eldest brother, named after a prince, Shahram, whom I adored. My family was jubilant over having a boy. Not that they were disappointed in having me as a firstborn—they were more modern than that. But they were thrilled to now have a boy and a girl. My grandmother Gohar, on my father's side, gave my mother a ruby pin when Shahram was born, but nothing was given to my mother when I arrived. Some Iranians live their lives in the past, where boys are the favored offspring. Shahram had the biggest pair of dark brown eyes. I treated him like he was my doll. He was very quiet, reserved, and shy, while I was beginning to show signs of being very outspoken, a trait that would follow me through life.

My brother Shahriar (meaning king) was born two years after Shahram and was a natural-born doctor. Nearly every summer, our parents would take us either to the country or the Caspian Sea, both almost four hours away from our home. We rented a house and took everything with us, including our rugs, mattresses, and pots and pans. It was like moving from one house to another. As my brothers and I played on the beach, I still remember young Shahriar dissecting dead frogs in the heat in order to study their anatomy. All the other kids would run to the emerald-colored sea, pick up seaweed, splash salty water, and chase one another in the thick sand, but Shahriar studied dead sea creatures on the beach for hours.

My third and last brother, Shahrokh ("face of a king"), was born ten years after me, in 1962.

When not renting a house, we stayed at the Caspian Sea

with my Aunt Badri, who loved gathering the whole family in her small two-bedroom villa. There were times when my cousins and I, more than fifteen of us, would sleep next to one another on the sofas, thin mattresses, and even a sheet covering the floor. We just wanted to be together. I remember how we marched by the sea in our imported American bathing suits and played volleyball on the beach well into our teens.

This was when we were young and restless and the world seemed magical and beautiful.

3

TEHRAN'S THINK TANK

M Y FATHER'S FATHER, Jahangir (meaning "world con-
queror"), was a handsome man, tall and slim, with a
pair of dark piercing eyes. When he read newspapers he wore a
monocle. He dressed in dark suits and white shirts, except in
the winter, when he wore thick dark jackets at home and read
all day long.

He loved discussing politics with his longtime friend and
neighbor, Professor Amir-Alaei, and Iran's most popular athlete
ever, Takhti, an Olympic wrestler. Takhti was in his early thirties. He was much younger than Grandpa and the professor,
but I assume he enjoyed their company and learned from them,
for he was quiet most of the time when they got together.
Grandpa and the professor talked at length. I know this because
I was there, too, and I, like Takhti, was a listener.

By the age of ten, I understood that our government suffered from a dictatorship under Shah Mohammed Reza Pahlavi's regime, but I innocently admired him. Since I couldn't see it unfolding on the streets in the small world that I lived in, going to these political sessions was an eye-opener for me, even if I didn't understand everything that they discussed.

Each time upon arrival, we were taken to the professor's huge library/home office. Grandpa and the professor were both pro Mosaddegh, the deposed prime minister of Iran who was then under house arrest. Although my youthful memories are murky, I feel they are important to set up the current history of Iran.

The Iranian Parliament voted unanimously in 1951 to nationalize the Iranian oil industry, which meant the government of Iran would keep the country's oil under its control and have the power to sell it to whomever they chose. This was all masterminded by the democratically elected nationalist movement and its prime minister, Dr. Mohammad Mosaddegh.

Nationalizing Iranian oil resulted in an annulment of the British and Iranian oil treaty. The Anglo-Iranian oil company had been under British control since 1913, with Iran earning only a small fraction of the revenue—even though the oil belonged to Iran. It was enormously beneficial to Britain's economy and political influence in the Middle East. Depriving Britain of its hugely profitable share of Iranian oil prompted the British to ask the Shah of Iran to remove Mosaddegh.

Even if it lasted less than a year, the nationalization of the oil industry was a sacred and popular act for the majority of Iranians. Only monarchists or pro-Shah followers were against it. (The Shah believed the oil made him popular with the Western world.) Nationalization put an end to hundreds of years of Iranian-oil exploitation by foreign powers. Removing its curator, Prime Minister Mosaddegh, would not be an easy task.

The Shah didn't have the backbone to remove the popular Mosaddegh in 1952. The British, with the Shah's knowledge, requested the help of America's CIA. Kermit Roosevelt Jr., an officer in the CIA and also a grandson of Theodore Roosevelt, was to carry out a coup in Iran code-named Operation Ajax. The plot was to overthrow Mosaddegh as prime minister and replace him with General Fazlollah Zahedi—who had previously been dismissed by Mosaddegh following a brutal attack on pro-nationalization protesters—by the order of the Shah and in agreement with both America and Britain. Despite careful planning, the first attempt failed, and the Shah had to flee Iran.

Mosaddegh was removed from power in 1953 by a second coup, planned and carried out by the CIA at the appeal of the British MI6, and staged by General Zahedi while the Shah was in exile in Rome.

Mosaddegh was arrested at his home on the night of August 19, 1953. The Shah returned to Iran on August 22.

Mosaddegh was detained and put on trial. He was sent to prison for three years and later put under house arrest until his death, in 1967.

When we made visits to the professor's house, Mosaddegh was still alive. Grandfather, the professor, and Takhti were appalled by Mosaddegh's humiliating arrest and his ludicrous trial and were hoping he would return to power even as the oil once again became a shared resource with other countries, including the U.S.A.

FOLLOWING MOSADDEGH'S ARREST, his supporters were tortured or executed. The minister of foreign affairs—his closest associate—was executed by order of the Shah's military court. Mosaddegh's followers had gone underground, and discussing his affairs was not permitted publicly, now that the Shah was back in power.

Grandpa and the professor would first close all the windows and draw the shutters, halfway. Takhti quietly sat on the chair next to the professor's desk. I sat in a hard-backed library chair against the professor's bookshelf, facing the window and absorbed by their very private conversations. The reflection of the sun formed horizontal lines of shadows on the professor's desk.

FOLLOWING AN ASSASSINATION attempt on the Shah, the main communist party of Iran, the pro-Soviet Tudeh Party, was banned. Up to fifty of its leaders were executed following the coup in 1953, with the help of Iran's secret police known as SAVAK, trained by the CIA. The fear of communism was a genuine concern of the progressive Iranians, and the Shah, a great ally of the U.S.A. in the region, was determined to keep the peace in the Middle East. Modernizing Iran and joining the Western world were the first two points on his agenda. That was his dream, but fate would intervene.

The Shah had studied in Europe and was influenced by Western culture. He went to school in Switzerland and was raised in a European environment. His first wife, Princess Fowzia Fuad of Egypt, was bright, educated, and charismatic. They married in 1939, and in 1940 she gave birth to a beautiful girl, Princess Shahnaz. Fowzia filed for divorce in 1945, claiming the Persian climate was hazardous to her health, and left Iran for good. It was really a political marriage.

Soraya Esfandiari Bakhtiari, the only daughter of an Iranian ambassador in Germany, was a statuesque beauty and married the Shah in 1951. They were very much in love, but he divorced her in 1958 because she was infertile. The Shah desperately needed a male heir, so he married his third wife, Farah Diba, in 1959. I still remember the day their royal wedding was aired on television. I was seven years old and was captivated by her beauty, her charming shy smile, and her regal wedding gown designed by Yves Saint Laurent at the House of Dior.

Farah was an attractive, tall athlete and an architecture student in Paris when she met the Shah at the Iranian embassy there. She loved Iran and loved to show off Iranian art and antiquities to the world. She was a great supporter of Iranian artists, too. Under her influence, Iran was becoming a hub of international artists, as well as a great cultural passage point between the East and the West. Not long after their marriage, she became pregnant and produced a male heir, Prince Reza.

The Shah was a proud and ambitious man. He spoke passionately of Iran's heritage and its enormous resources. He was particularly proud of the fact that the first Declaration of Human Rights was written by Cyrus the Great, in ancient Iran, known as Babylon, in 539 B.C. The Shah also spoke of change, but, as the professor and my grandfather said, he was a delusional man. He refused to see the reality that Iranians were not ready for modernization and were stuck in old religious indoctrinations and ancient traditions.

His so-called White Revolution gave Iranian women the

right to vote in 1963 and was one of his series of reforms. He also personally handed out the deeds of land parcels to hundreds of peasants, making them landlords. The White Revolution was his first of many attempts to help the country realize its great potential and to modernize. While my grandfather and the professor thought some of the reforms were good, they still felt strongly that Iran should be an independent country without Western influences.

The Shah promised Iranians that he would take them to "the gates of a great civilization" if they stood by him, but it was a wish that never came true.

Iran had become a police state under the fearsome SAVAK, which reported to the Shah. Despite reforms, the lack of democracy and political freedom had turned Iran into a claustrophobic society. People feared their own shadows, had a hard time trusting one another, and feared torture for saying something that might make SAVAK hunt them down.

SAVAK was merciless and had zero tolerance for any inclination to any political party other than the Shah's. It was a one-party political system. Scholars, artists, and academics were randomly interrogated for publicly criticizing the Shah's regime. Student activists were taken to jail, and the number of young, so-called political prisoners was said to have been rising. When the professor and my grandfather spoke of this in low voices, Takhti and I looked at each other. In truth, I was scared.

I REMEMBER WHERE I was when I learned that U.S. president John F. Kennedy had been shot. I was in the fifth grade at the Fatiah Girls School in Tehran. Around 10:00 A.M. the faculty called all of the students out to the courtyard. Around two hundred of us assembled and were told the news. We were asked to pray for President Kennedy. To us, he represented a true American: optimistic, determined, and young and handsome.

In fact he seemed too young to be called the father of a nation, but his smile was fatherly and heartwarming. His pictures with his family were all over Iranian magazines. Iranians particularly thought his wife, Jacqueline, was the most beautiful and chic woman in the world. Her haircut was something our mothers copied at their hairdressers.

My grandfather and the professor were worried about what would happen to the United States and the relationship between the two countries, which during the Kennedy years was very good. Kennedy respected Iran as an equal. Now what?

America in my young eyes was a faraway land, a vast country with spectacular scenery, as shown in American films and westerns. Yet despite these dramatic depictions, it seemed like a peaceful place where people's dreams came true. America was said to have a real democracy. It was a young country, full of endless ambition. The fact that the First Amendment guarantees the freedom of speech stunned my generation, having overheard horrifying stories of people losing their lives over exercising their freedom of speech in Iran.

For as long as I could remember, there were certain subjects we could not speak about publicly. We couldn't publicly criticize the Shah and his family or discuss communism or certain books, which were banned from our young eyes, including *The Little Red Book* by the leader of the Chinese revolution, Chairman Mao Tse-tung, and Marx's *The Communist Manifesto*. In general, all books related to communism or socialism were banned. The list was quite long.

Just like my grandfather, my father taught us as much as he could about politics. Father was an avid listener of the BBC, which was broadcast in Iran under the radar. All he wanted was for us to be good people and to educate ourselves. Both of my parents were in agreement with that.

My sessions with the threesome ended when my grandfather died. Then, in 1968, when Takhti was thirty-six, he allegedly committed suicide, but it was rumored that the government killed him for his liberal political beliefs. Even today, I miss all of them dearly and feel that being around them, even if it was just to soak in their knowledge, was where the seeds of my rebellion were sown.

4

THAT ACTING BUG

DESPITE MY FASCINATION with politics, I developed a love for acting, even if it was only to perform in front of my little cousins. I had never thought of acting as a realistic career choice. My parents had always encouraged my siblings and me to attend university, and my father was intent that I should become a doctor. Still, it was fun to pretend.

Staying at Grandma Bahar al-Sadat's house during the summer had many advantages. One of them was my cousin Nasrin, Uncle Sadr's daughter, who lived in the adjoining court-yard. She was, and still is, like an older sister to me. She and I would select neighboring kids and demand that they sit in Nasrin's front yard, where we performed short plays for them during long hot afternoons. We were older, so they knew they could not move from their seats on the stairs without risking our wrath. Nasrin made up the stories, and I took care of the costumes, hair, and makeup.

My beautiful Aunt Afsar—my mom's sister and a true fan of Jayne Mansfield—was tall and slim with milky white skin and dark blond hair. She visited Grandma regularly and offered us her surplus lipsticks, which we recycled as blush. Grandma used kohl on her inner eyelids: *sormeh*, a powder made of burnt chestnut shells, in a small silver jar. We would also line our eyes with it to look like Elizabeth Taylor in *Cleopatra*.

We begged Nasrin's mother, Aunt Maryam, to lend us some of her clothes. She was fairly tall for an Iranian but thin, perhaps a size two. She was chic, bearing a slight resemblance to Olivia de Havilland. She made her own dresses out of fine imported fabrics and was inspired mostly by Hollywood and movie stars like Joan Crawford and Bette Davis.

Nasrin's short plays revolved around a mother and daughter quarreling over the girl's lifestyle. She always played the mother and I portrayed her outspoken, outgoing, and modern-thinking daughter.

I was visiting Nasrin and her family in Canada a few years ago when she asked me, "How come you always got to play the modern daughter and I played the submissive mother?"

I said, "Sweetheart, you were the writer of those shows, remember? You wrote those parts." We both laughed our hearts out.

5

THE HIJINKS OF GOLDIE

A T AGE FIFTEEN, I was allowed to go out with my friends in the early evenings. I liked to entertain my friends by imitating them and famous actresses. We would go to the Paramount Theater, a lavish theater in the heart of Tehran and architecturally reminiscent of the European theaters I saw in movies. That afternoon they were premiering *Cactus Flower*, starring the strikingly beautiful, and refreshingly funny, Goldie Hawn, alongside Walter Matthau and Ingrid Bergman.

After the movie was over, we were all out on the street, deciding where to go next. I was imitating Goldie, and my friends were laughing. I suddenly lost control of my body and fell hard to the pavement on my left side. I tried to get up immediately to avoid further embarrassment, but I could not move my legs.

My friends put me in a cab and took me home. I was diagnosed with a severe heart ailment known as rheumatic fever.

Our family doctor suggested complete bed rest and large doses of penicillin, including daily injections.

My father exhausted every avenue at the Ministry of Health, where he was now in a leadership role, to take me to the country's best and most well known heart hospital, which was located outside Tehran, near the holy city of Qom. The head of the hospital, Dr. Saleh, had graduated from Boston University in Massachusetts.

I was moved to the hospital for a week and left alone for the first time in my life. I could not have visitors, except for my parents, who could visit only once a day and stay for only thirty minutes. The doctor said I should not get out of bed and should not get excited under any circumstances. I could not watch TV nor listen to the radio. I could not even read books or magazines. The nurses were really nice and injected a high dose of penicillin into my body, four times a day, starting at dawn. I despised the hospital and cried my eyes out, no matter how friendly the staff was.

But I did love the view from my room. That was all I had to distract me. The tips of tall trees, against the vast sky, displayed an unimaginable variety of colors. The sky was cobalt blue at dawn, and then turned into a light, satin blue later in the morning. It was pure gold at noon, emerging into a rainbow of bright colors right before sunset, ranging from dark orange to dark purple, then changing into gray, which finally gave way to the darkness of night.

I often imagined myself at a huge welcome-home party with all my family and friends at my side. I wished I could go back in time and sit on Grandma's lap, feel her warmth, and hear her melodic voice making up stories to keep me seated. I imagined myself dressed elaborately in white chiffon next to my husband, passionately in love with me. He did not have a face yet, but I could see a pair of loving eyes smiling at me. Then I dreamed of designing my wedding dress, drawing imaginary lines in the air, choosing the right fabric in my mind, picturing the final result.

Finally I was sent home, but under one condition: I had to be cared for by a trained nurse in a similar environment. The second floor of our house was turned into my nursing headquarters. My bed was in the middle of the main living room, the largest room in the house.

Being at home was almost heavenly compared to being in the hospital. My brothers went to school during the day and came to see me afterward. I still could not watch TV and was dying to find out if Dr. Richard Kimble, in *The Fugitive*, had been captured yet. My brothers and I watched it religiously. *The Fugitive* was our favorite TV series, and I had missed a lot of episodes. I talked to my brothers and promised them that I would not get excited if they briefed me on the story each week, so after every episode, they would sneak into my room and give me the good news that the fugitive was still at large, looking for his wife's killer, the one-armed man.

Miss Susan, my literature teacher, had told my parents that she would help tutor me and came over every other day. She was beautiful and extremely kind, just like in fairy tales. Her visits gave me the hope of returning to school, though I was told that I would have to repeat the grade the following year. I did not mind. All I wanted was to walk again and to live life to its fullest.

After eight months, I was well enough to get on my feet and was told to take short walks. My cousins came over to take me for my first one, through the alley to my favorite cozy café, Paris, where they served coffee with pastries. I left the house, dragging my feet on the ground and holding on to my cousin's arms. Everything seemed new to me. It was the same alley, but somehow it looked different—it was that much more beautiful. In fact, I loved everything about life and its creatures at that very moment when I started walking again.

The alley was covered in yellow jasmines, climbing up the brick walls in the spring. The scent of yellow jasmines in my nostrils and the last rays of the sun, glistening through the branches of the trees, made me want to live more than at any other time in my life.

Life becomes meaningful in comparison only. I did not know how lucky I was until I had experienced the sorrow of the hospital.

AFTER I WAS well on my feet, we went to my Uncle Jalal's ranch in northern Iran. He was a landowner and merchant who owned acres of cotton fields. Jalal and his family lived in a ranch close to a little town called Bandare-Gaz. His wife, whom we called "Auntie," was a kind, generous, and pious woman. She wore a scarf around her face in the presence of men. She did not make her daughters do the same. They had nine children, six girls and three boys. My uncle was traveling most of the time; therefore the burden of raising the children in a small town fell on Auntie's shoulders. The girls were well mannered, fun, giggly, and pure. They were similar to the girls in *Pride and Prejudice* or *Sense and Sensibility*, with the same lifestyle and environment. My brothers and I loved visiting them, and thankfully they loved having us.

Uncle Jalal would pick us up from the train station and take us to the ranch in a big old Chevy. Once there, my brothers would run off with our male cousins and I would immerse myself in my female cousins' world. We would wake up early and run around the vegetable and herb gardens in the huge backyard. We were free to pick our favorite edibles but had to wash them thoroughly in the cold, luminous water of the valve in the front yard.

Still a tomboy, I loved joining the boys in their activities, which included hanging out by the train tracks. We would place our bodies straight out on the ground, put our heads on the rail, and listen carefully for the whistling sound of the approaching trains, trying to figure out how far off they were.

AUNTIE PROMISED TO take us to the only movie theater in the town to see a special screening of *Gone With the Wind*, but first we had to visit with her fabric vendor who was coming with fine imported fabrics. Most of them were imported from Russia. The girls and I were all over the fabrics and kept asking the merchant for tips on fashion, as if he worked for *Vogue*.

"What is the 'in' color this year?"

"What is out of fashion this season?"

The poor vendor had no clue what we were talking about and kept telling us that he didn't know, all the while assuring us they were the "finest fabrics" and "made for princesses."

We went to the theater right after he left and were a bit late for the movie; the lights had just gone down. Auntie and Mom sat us in the middle and *Gone With the Wind* started. I had never seen anything like it before. This was definitely larger than life, let alone larger than cinema.

The grandeur of the scenes, elaborately shot, had given birth to an epic, which not only blew my teenage mind away but also stayed with me for years to come.

I was mesmerized by Scarlett's love, perseverance, self-righteousness, and feistiness. I was puzzled by Ashley's state of denial and taken by Melanie's selflessness and endearing qualities. Finally, I was furious at Rhett Butler for being such a heartless, foolish man. (Never mind how my perception of the film has changed throughout the years, to the point where I now see that Scarlett is the heartless and selfish character, and not Rhett, who is truly in love with her.)

Watching it then, in the modest town theater, made a huge impact on me. I realized how much I wanted to become a serious actress. Before I went to sleep that evening, to the sound of chirping crickets, I made a vow. I promised myself that I was going to become an actress, no matter what, and to name my daughter, if I were lucky enough to have one, after Scarlett's heritage: Tara.

6

FATIMA'S WARNING

DESPITE ALL THE air pollution caused by the newly built factories around town, and despite surveillance of the SAVAK unit looking for student activists, my generation enjoyed what seemed like a period of stability in Iran. Tehran was growing fast. Tall apartment buildings were being erected here and there. The architecture around the city was becoming more eclectic. Georgian mansions would lie next door to scaled-down versions of America's White House. The new town was being built around the old town. It was hectic to drive. God forbid you didn't remember how to get to a friend's place.

YEARS AGO, EVERY time Nasrin and I wanted to go out and play hopscotch in the alley, Fatima would appear from nowhere, warning us that we should not go out unaccompanied. She said Tehran was not safe, but we didn't believe her.

"Don't you understand?" she would say. "Trafficking gangs will cover your heads with potato sacks and will sell you for one Ashrafi [a gold coin] at the gulf and you will never see your homeland or your family again."

Fatima never forgot the past, but somehow she never allowed her ill-fated destiny to take away her kindness and her love for humanity.

A FRIEND OF my father's told him that it would be wise for us teenagers to become familiar with computers, and so my father took me to after-school classes. He thought it would be a good idea for me to start studying computer science and learn typing in order to help me become a doctor. I studied the COBOL programming language and keypunching. I was discovering a new world and its codes. I was enthralled. In retrospect, it felt like watching James Cameron's *Avatar* for the first time. There was no doubt that computers were the future and working with them would prepare me for my higher education.

The computer classes were held in the late afternoon until the early evening, right after school. I then made the fifteen-minute walk home through the neighborhood at six o'clock, which was sunny and fun during the spring and the summer, but became dark and scary in the winter.

One January evening, I had taken longer to gather my belongings and left the school much later than the others. The school alley was empty when I got out of the building, and everybody was gone. It was dark, and a couple of tall and narrow lampposts were the only source of light.

I was wrapped in heavy winter clothing, and the alley was

blanketed in snow. I could barely see ahead, but I kept walking and turned onto the main street when I noticed a car, a Volkswagen, moving slowly near me. I slowed down and kept a keen eye on it. The car stopped, and the man next to the driver got out. I started walking as fast as I could in the heavy snow, but he grabbed my shoulders and held my hands tight behind me. Fighting for my life, I kicked him hard in the crotch with my winter boots. He let go of me and grabbed himself in pain. Then the driver got out, and I shouted "Help!" at the top of my lungs.

The two men were forcing me into their car when I heard a policeman whistling. It was a miracle. He came from out of nowhere and was not even on his post. He just happened to be on his way home. The kidnappers jumped into their car and left me in the middle of the street. The policeman took me home, and when my father saw me with him, he knew something bad had happened. My brothers were furious, and the neighborhood was in shock. Fatima soon learned of the incident and told every single detail to every child in my family, no matter what their age. She said to me, "Shohreh, you are the lucky one."

My parents were devastated, but there was nothing we could do. My father asked me if I still wanted to go back to school. My brothers were younger than me and took a bus from school straight home and my father worked till late at the ministry, so I had no one to walk me home. I immediately said yes. If there is one thing that I have learned from my father, it is "Success can only be achieved if you overcome fear."

7

VOGUE

I WAS SIXTEEN years old when my mother's hairdresser asked her to allow me to model in his hair fashion show at his salon. My hair was long and thick, and he loved experimenting with it by creating fancy updo hairstyles.

Knowing that it was just a small and private affair for his clientele helped my mother in her decision to accept the offer.

I was so exited the night before, going through my mother's fashion magazines, including Germany's *Burda* style magazine (with enclosed sewing patterns) and *Elle*. I studied the models and tried to imitate how they posed: standing tall with their right foot slightly ahead of their left, hands on their waist, or gently resting on their lapels. Then I cut out my favorite pictures and stacked and flicked through them. The images started moving, just like the animation in a flip book. Browsing through the pages fast brought the pictures to life.

I wore a nice white silk-chiffon minidress that my mother had bought for me in London, where she would go once a year to visit relatives and to shop. My hair was styled up, and the hairdresser added a chiffon headband to it. His makeup artist did his best to make me look like Jean Shrimpton because she believed I was too overweight to resemble Twiggy. The two models were wildly popular in Iran for their exceptional beauty and were featured prominently in Iranian magazines and *Elle*.

Jean was well known for her look, her feminine curvy body, and for being one of the world's supermodels. Twiggy was acknowledged as the most beautiful skinny girl in the world and had the longest eyelashes. Little did we know, her eyelashes were fake. But the secret came out soon, and Iranian ladies demanded that little extra beauty for themselves, too.

The salon was transformed into a hair-fashion studio. Rows of twenty-four chairs were neatly placed along a short runway in the middle of the salon.

I walked the red carpet like I owned it, my mother said. She was amazed at my self-confidence and surprised to see my showmanship. She asked me, "Shohreh, how did you manage to walk and pose in front of the people and not get intimidated?"

"I loved it," I said. "I was playing the role of a model."

A YEAR LATER my schoolmate Pari-Sima, the niece of the regal couturier Parvin, encouraged me to hit the catwalk, along with a couple of European models, at a private reception held at Parvin's prestigious boutique.

I was afraid to ask my parents' permission, knowing they

would most likely not let me model there. They were very private people and did not like their children to show off. My father had made it clear that he did not want me to act or to see me on a stage, period. I was to be a doctor.

So I went behind their backs and went to see Mrs. Parvin at her couture house, known as Mari-Martin. She was tall, slim, and elegant. She spoke softly and walked quietly.

There were flowers everywhere, planted in large crystal vases, tall white lilies and white tuberoses, known as Gole Maryam (or the Saint Mary flower) in Iran. The whole boutique was designed in white and eggshell colors, except for its early-twentieth-century French chandeliers with twelve citron shades, and two small antique Persian rugs.

Parvin invited me to join her models and walk the runway at her upcoming couture show at the boutique. I was thrilled, but I had to quickly learn the basics of the so-called catwalk.

A German ex-model catwalk expert and modeling instructor named Ralph was hired to work with the models. I told my parents I was studying at my friend Pari-Sima's but went to the boutique instead. I worked with Ralph while Pari-Sima helped her aunt with the guest list and invitations for the upcoming fashion show.

I worked hard to walk straight on the line Ralph had marked for me on the floor. I was in awe of all the French silks, beads, rayon, stones, chiffons, and colored laces in royal blue, green, and dark red, ready to be sewn into gowns for the show.

Ralph was pretty tough; he constantly made me practice walking a straight line. Then he asked me to put my hands on my hips and walk the line again. He was merciless.

I could not understand a word he was saying. He did not speak Farsi and I did not speak German or English. Pari-Sima translated his words as he acted them out for me.

Ralph turned blue with frustration as he tried to teach me not to think of anything while walking the runway. I was to be a blank slate, and I am a woman with many thoughts!

As I practiced, he noticed that I was landing on my heels first and not my toes. I told him my father said I walked like an army of soldiers. He laughed then bent my foot, pushing my toes down. Then he held my heel. Eventually and miraculously, Ralph taught me how to gracefully walk the floor. He did his best to teach me as much as he could in a couple of sessions, and I did my best to hold my own alongside the European models at the show.

I finally decided to tell my mother the secret. She said she did not like the idea, but she understood my situation, having promised Parvin I would do it. I asked her to go with me, and she said she would rather not. I guess this was her way of making me feel responsible for my choices rather than sharing them with me.

The success of the show convinced a well-known Iranian designer, Pouran Daroodi, to offer me the sum of a hundred toman (fifteen dollars) to walk the runway in her upcoming private show.

She said I was the same size as the Queen of Iran. Pouran had designed a few evening dresses with the queen in mind, and she wanted me to introduce them on the runway. She was very excited about her new collection and arranged for me to start my fittings immediately.

The fittings took place twice a week for a month. To spend that much time at the salon was more than I was allowed to spend outside my home. I begged my mother to let me go to the fittings, which lasted several hours each time. She was not very keen on the idea, but I could tell she was secretly as excited as I was. She too liked participating in social activities. By now she was thirty-eight years old and an active member of our community. She was a member of the Women's Club of Knowledge; she studied English and played bridge with other women her age. She even participated in the club's yearly poetry competition and once won a beautiful white summer umbrella with large prints of peonies in pink and light green for reciting one of Rumi's poems.

My mother was and still is an avid reader, mostly of novels, and a movie lover as well. She truly enjoys talking about each book or film for days and weeks at a time. She loves the Brontë sisters, and *Wuthering Heights*, *Rebecca*, and *Anna Karenina* are her favorite films. She loved Clark Gable and Vivien Leigh. She also adored Elizabeth Taylor.

Knowing the show was private and for women only, she gave me her blessing. I was allowed to keep my first earnings. Still, she preferred that we keep the secret between the two of us. She said I should know that this would be my last walk on the runway and reminded me that I was sixteen years old, no longer a child, and had to respect my parents' wish for me, which was of course to be a doctor.

I had no intention of undertaking modeling as a profession. I wanted to be an actor and loved just walking on the stage. So I agreed. I didn't tell my mother my dreams of acting, even as my parents were actively planning to send me to Germany for medical school.

Pouran's atelier was adjacent to her house on a shady street in an old but prominent area of Tehran. During our sessions, she had me stand on a pedestal for hours and talked to me about the fashion industry in Paris and Iran. It was her belief that Iran was nothing less than Paris in the fashion world. Pouran stood there, watching the look of her preliminary designs on me. Her assistants pinned the lining patterns, used as a guide for every single dress or gown, on my body. She was meticulous with her designs. She oversaw every detail in the light of the sun, which poured into the room through the garden windows.

The fashion show was eventually held in a rich family's opulent backyard in northern Tehran. A runway was installed right under the cypress trees, planted neatly in a row.

Princess Maingeh, the wife of Prince Gholam-reza, the Shah's brother, was coming to the show as well. I met Farzaneh Malek, a famous Iranian couturier, who was becoming a celebrity in the Iranian fashion world. She asked if I would be able to work with her, too, and I told her I would have to ask my parents first.

POURAN'S EVENING GOWNS were elaborately made out of fine imported French fabrics and were mostly beaded with semiprecious stones, creating a rainbow of pastel colors. She also loved appliquéd gowns. She mixed and matched fabrics, with black lace on white satin, or pieces of antique Iranian fabrics sewn to the royal-looking gowns.

I became worried when I saw a couple of photographers at

the arrival area. I was told that they were the house photographers, even though this was supposed to be a private event. But since Princess Maingeh was attending, they had to have at least one media outlet. A journalist from *Etelaat*, Iran's favorite daily newspaper, had also come with a photographer.

All the other models were wondering why I was so upset by the presence of the cameras. They had no idea I was doing this behind my father's back. But by midafternoon the show had started and I was on the runway, being photographed!

I got home early, still worried about the pictures, but did not say anything to my mother. My father was a subscriber to *Etelaat*. He looked forward to reading it every evening. I told my brothers to watch for the newspaper.

When I returned home after school the following day, I was mortified to see a head-to-toe photograph of me in Pouran's evening gown on the cover. It took up almost a quarter of the page. I was speechless.

My brothers were concerned. Shahriar suggested that we hide the paper and tell Dad it had never come that day. Shahram thought it was a stupid idea. Dad could still go to the newsstand around the corner and buy one.

"What if the newsstand ran out of it?" asked Shahriar. We asked him what he meant, and he said, "Why not buy all the papers on the stand?"

"But there are two of them," said Shahram.

He was right. There were two newsstands on the corner. But we could still do it. We put our savings together, and Shahriar and I went to both corner stands and bought up all the papers. Thanks to the popularity of the newspaper, there were not a lot left. We stacked them all in the attic and retreated to our rooms, anticipating our father's return.

When he came home, he asked for the newspaper as soon as he'd brewed his dark tea.

We lied and said we had no idea where it was. He did not say anything but was obviously not convinced.

A half hour later, he summoned all of us to join him and my mother in the living room. He stood in the middle of the room with the paper in his hand. He had picked it up at the barbershop next to the newsstand, after he could not find his. We had thought about the newsstands but had forgotten the barbershop. Shahriar and I exchanged a quick look. Shahram was mortified. My youngest brother, Shahrokh, was too young to understand what was going on.

My father then said that he had known about the fashion shows I had participated in from the very beginning. I should have known better, as my parents never hid anything from each other. They were not just an ordinary husband and wife; they were true lovers and treated each other as such. All this time he knew it but had not said anything. He did not mind my harmless adventures, but he didn't want me to get hooked on modeling, either.

He said I looked stunning in the picture. "Very ladylike," he said. He also liked what the reporter had said about me: "Iranian models are breaking through." He then told me that having fun is necessary but that higher education is a necessity, especially in the twentieth century.

He looked at me, taking a long, deliberate pause, and said, "Do you think Queen Elizabeth would ever do such a thing? I mean modeling?"

My father was obsessed with Queen Elizabeth II of England and tried to bring her into every conversation that concerned dignity and class.

After my picture was published, I was bombarded with offers from well-known designers to follow up with my modeling. But I had to put them all on hold until was eighteen and I could figure things out for myself.

8

THE ERA OF SWEET DREAMS

TEHRAN WAS CALLED the Paris of the Middle East. This was in the late sixties. My friends and I hung out at the bowling alley; the Ice Palace, a vast two-story modern-looking skating club with a large indoor skating rink; the Iran-America Society, which included film retrospectives; and a German cultural institute that often hosted small European New Age concerts. Additionally there were a handful of sidewalk cafés on Tehran's most popular boulevard strip, called Pahlavi, after the Shah, whom I would meet around this time.

My friend the designer Farzaneh Malek asked me to accompany her and two others to the palace to model for the queen. When we arrived it was just the queen, Farah Diba, her dame of honor, and her mother. After the modeling was finished, the queen asked us to stay for dinner. We ate rice with cherries and saffron-flavored chicken. It was served very informally, and we were all at ease. I guess that is why most Iranians called her "the people's queen." She was very humble and kind.

The king suddenly entered the room with his entourage. He looked dashing in his slick suit and wore a confident smile at all times. When the tea was served, he invited us to join him on the balcony. It was a calm and serene night. The lights of the city were racing with the light shining from the stars. We stood in a line facing the glorious view of Tehran, and the king said to us, "We've come this far to modernize Iran. Look at what you see. I won't stop until it's complete." Then he turned his head, looked into our eyes, and said, "I am so proud of us." Despite what Grandfather and the professor had said about his dictatorial regime, I admired this man who loved our country so much.

I guess the best way to convey my feelings for him at the time is that fascism has its own charisma. The concept is beautifully portrayed in the movie *Lust, Caution*, directed by Ang Lee and based on a short story by the Chinese writer Eileen Chang. Set mostly in the early 1940s in Japanese-occupied Shanghai, a university drama student involved in an assassination plot of a Fascist collaborator falls in love with the collaborator.

There were also tea dancing clubs, where we paid a dollar and a half for a cup of tea and a piece of cake and danced to the latest popular music, including James Brown, Tom Jones, the Beatles, Janis Joplin, and Shirley Bassey and her song "I Who Have Nothing." We danced from 4:00 to 7:00 P.M. on Thursdays only, the last day of the work week in Iran. We could not get too close to each other when we tangoed, because the monitors would intervene and ask us to leave.

Last but not least were Thursday's premieres of the latest European and American films. Iran's Radio City Theatre started the trend, and other theaters soon followed. Every Thursday night, hundreds of young faces turned out. Tickets were purchased during the week, and they were sold out by the actual day. You couldn't even buy them on the black market, which shows you how popular these premieres were.

Young people with hungry minds would socialize and spend hours discussing the movies afterward in the nearby sidewalk cafés.

I WAS ALMOST nineteen years old when I met my first serious suitor. It was right after I graduated from high school. I was at a friend's house and the host had told me that a gentleman named Aydin Aghdashloo was coming. Aydin had just returned from England. He was thirty-one, soft-spoken, and handsome, with white porcelain skin, light brown hair, and bluish—or maybe greenish—eyes. (I could never tell their true color.) He was half Russian and half Turkish-Iranian.

When introduced by the host, Aydin politely sat next to me and started asking all sorts of questions regarding my school, my parents, and my life in Iran. I was fascinated by his knowledge and his command of Farsi, the rich, melodic, and ancient Persian language.

When dinner was ready to be served, I waited for the host's seating assignment.

Finally, she uttered the words: "Why don't you sit next to Aydin? It seems like you have a lot in common."

A FEW WEEKS later Aydin called at our home. My mother came to my room, eyes wide. She said that Aydin had asked her permission to take me to an early dinner. She was delighted to have talked with him, and I guess she was even more delighted that someone had enough class to ask a girl's parents for their consent.

Three days later he appeared at our door in a light brown Yves Saint Laurent cotton suit, holding two white orchids beautifully set into a small green vase. He kissed my mother's hand and stepped inside our house. He was very European.

The notoriously hot summer days in Tehran had arrived, and the café restaurants on Pahlavi Boulevard, such as Chattanooga and Sorrento, were my favorites. I adored Chattanooga for its huge half-moon-shaped seating area facing the boulevard, and Sorrento for its jukebox that for one toman (ten cents) played my favorite song, "If You Go Away," sung by Shirley Bassey.

We went to Chattanooga. I wanted to become Aydin's friend and get him to consider marrying one of my cousins who was looking for a husband—ideally a very handsome one.

My mind was so occupied by my parents' wish that I become a doctor that I refused to see the possibility of getting engaged. I was also thinking that I should be in England studying acting (I had an aunt who lived there), but I was afraid of losing my family over it. I kept focused on my cousin's case, and Aydin kept talking about the clash of romanticism, idealism, and pragmatism. Aydin believed all humans are equal and ought to be treated equally. I could not have agreed with him more.

When I asked him why he left Europe and chose to live in

Iran instead, he said his real passion was to paint and that he enjoyed working for an Iranian advertising company as a graphic designer and an illustrator.

"I get inspired by people, nature, the atmosphere and rich colors in the fruits, carpets, and rugs of this country. My inspiration comes from the colors of the pomegranates, grapes, vegetables, the thousands of different shades of green, brown, and gold in the autumn, and of course the emerald green of the Caspian Sea. I cannot live anywhere else," he said. "Nor will I ever."

OUR SECOND DATE was a week later at one of the most "in" places in Tehran. The Labyrinth was a nice, cool hangout divided by cozy booths, which formed a semilabyrinth. It was a favorite spot of young people during the hot summer days. The walls were painted blue and white, which caused them to sparkle under the hidden dim yellow lights above.

For our second date, Aydin wore a creamy white cotton suit like Dirk Bogarde in Visconti's *Death in Venice*. We talked for an hour or two, covering all subjects. He was observing me, watching me carefully from every angle, and asked many questions.

He wanted to know if I was dating anyone, and I told him I'd promised my father I would study in Germany now that I had graduated. Aydin told me that I would be far better off living in Iran than anywhere else.

We switched to talking about our interests, and I was stunned by his knowledge of films. He admired the Italian masters like Federico Fellini, Pier Paolo Pasolini, and Vittorio De Sica. He was in awe of John Huston and also loved watching French film noir.

I was listening, absorbing every word like a sponge. The more he described and analyzed the films that I had seen but missed their hidden meanings, the more I realized how naive and illiterate I had been.

Aydin asked me to meet him at the Iran-America Society the next week and watch *The Seventh Seal* at the Ingmar Bergman retrospective. The Iran-America Society was a cultural center that promoted Western art and literature, mostly American. Its large concrete building consisted of a big theater, used for stage and screen presentations, a painting gallery, an exhibition room, a café, and a few lecture rooms.

I had taken a cab and was feeling anxious, putting my makeup on in the taxi because my father was against it. "Again you dip your head in a bucket of flour," he would say. "You don't need it. Youth is beautiful."

The Seventh Seal was beyond my comprehension, and Aydin did his best to crack its codes for me with examples from the Bible.

The following week I decided to challenge him by giving him a cultural shock in his own country. I took him to one of my favorite discos, Chandelier, off of Pahlavi Boulevard. It was lavishly decorated with a touch of Tudor style, combining red velvets with thick wooden furniture and a dozen antique chandeliers.

We sat in a corner so we would be able to talk. Neither of us drank alcoholic beverages. I started talking about my cousin Homa as soon as I got my virgin margarita and told him that she would be a perfect match for him. He smiled and changed the subject.

At the end of the night, while taking me home in a cab, he hastily mentioned that he was not interested in meeting my cousin. He said he was seriously interested in me. I could see the taxi driver's face in the mirror and his big grin at Aydin proposing marriage right there in the cab.

He added that he was aware of the age difference between us but was not alarmed. He thought I was more mature than my age. He asked me to think about his proposal.

I was speechless. I knew he was interested in me but foolishly thought that I could convince him to marry my cousin. Then again, maybe I knew deep down that this moment would arrive.

The following week I was lost, torn between an unknown future in Germany and a life with a man whom I would never get tired of speaking to or run out of subjects to talk about.

He was ready to get married, but I on the other hand did not intend for things to move so quickly. Germany was calling. A friend of my father's had done a search in Munich and found a nice Iranian family to take care of me. But I was not ready for this journey yet either. Acting was the love of my life and all I wanted to do was to study it. I could hardly stand still next to an ill person, let alone tend to one. Nevertheless, acting was out of the question. My mother had made it clear that I should not think or talk about acting while living under my parents' roof. Acting, especially acting in films, was not well thought of at the time, and proper families would not allow their daughters to pursue it.

My mother said, "This is not Switzerland, young lady—this is Iran. Your father would never agree to it." Mother genuinely believed that the Swiss were the most civilized people in the world. But to my parents, there was no life beyond their roof in Iran except higher education.

The fact was that Aydin was a perfect suitor for a girl my age, offering a progressive life in a traditional country. But would he be able to understand my love for acting?

I phoned him a few days later and asked him to meet me at Chattanooga again. This time I did not waste time. "Aydin, if we get married, will you let me follow my dream and become an actor?" I asked.

He was surprised by what he was hearing. Looking at me in astonishment, he said, "I am afraid it would be totally wrong of me to go through with the marriage with you for the wrong reason. Do you want to marry me or to become an actress?"

I said both. I told him that I needed to make sure that I would be able to follow my dreams or I would never be fully happy.

"Shohreh," he said, "I do not see why you should not follow your dream and pursue acting." I could not believe my ears.

"Do you really mean it? Will you really let me become an actor?"

"Yes. You have my word."

My father was shocked when I told him that I had decided to marry Aydin. (I gave him half of the news, skipping the acting part.) All he managed to say was, "Alas, I did my best for you to become a doctor and you chose to be a housewife."

TWO MONTHS LATER, in June 1971, we were married. One hundred and fifty guests gathered in an exotic fruit orchard. The wedding was catered by Moby Dick restaurant, named after

Melville's classic novel. They served a five-course dinner. The guests sat at tables around the rose garden, entertained by musicians playing Persian wedding songs.

My wedding gown was bought from a private seller working out of her home. It was simple yet rich with its embroideries and pinkish hue. It came with a matching tiara.

My aunt insisted that I go to her hairdresser and make the color of my hair a shade lighter, which I did. But the hairdresser could not make my hair lighter without it becoming reddish in color. So the end result was orange blond. I did not have time to argue, nor to cry. I was already late for the first part of the wedding, called the *aghd*. This is the traditional wedding ceremony, which has to take place before sunset at the bride's house in the presence of a cleric and the elders of the family.

As bride and groom, we sat on short-legged stools covered with soft red-velvet cushions, facing the colorful embroidered silk-chiffon tablecloth that lay over the carpet. There was a pair of matching crystal candelabras on each side of a leaning seventeenth-century mirror my aunt had given us, surrounded by matching dishes filled with sweets. Flatbreads in silver trays were decorated with flowers, nuts, and tiny pearls—all symbols of prosperity, wealth, and health—and placed in front of the mirror to create the reflective image of eternal love.

My mother had designed the whole theme, and she was very happy with the result. She loved the fact that I was no longer talking about acting. My father did everything in his power to turn the night into a memorable one for me.

Aydin looked stunning in his Piero de Monzi dark brown velvet suit and impressed all the members of my family, especially the female ones, who kept telling me how lucky I was to have found him. My cousin Homa jokingly said, "I thought you had him in mind for me?"

"I did my best," I said. "But it was not meant to be." We both laughed.

Everyone danced under the stars all night until dawn.

The next day, I moved all of my belongings to the small apartment that Aydin had rented for us. He used to live with his mother and thought it would be best for us to be on our own and have some privacy. But I knew that somehow I would bring his mom to live with us soon. She was an elegant lady, with a fairly dramatic background. She came from a distinguished Turkish family and had married Aydin's father, a Russian, who in the early 1900s had crossed the Aras River along the border with Turkey to live in Iran, like so many expats who'd fled the Russian Revolution.

The couple had a great life in Iran near the Caspian Sea, socializing mostly with aristocratic Russian immigrants. But at age ten, fate took Aydin's father away from him, when he suddenly passed away. Since his father's family were all in the Soviet Union, Aydin and his mother moved to Tehran to be closer to her relatives.

AYDIN AND I lived in a two-bedroom apartment on the second floor of a two-story complex on Kakh Avenue, in the heart of Tehran, near the prime minister's headquarters and within walking distance of my parents' new apartment. (They had decided to sell our old home, as they no longer needed the space to impress a suitor for their daughter.) Our complex belonged to a friend of Aydin's, a renowned critic and writer who lived on the first floor with his beautiful wife.

We were getting ready for our honeymoon in Lebanon and Algeria, when Aydin told me that a friend of his, Fraydoon-Ave, a painter and an art designer who worked with the City Theatre, had mentioned something about the Theatre Workshop of Tehran's auditions for its upcoming play *Narrow Road to the Deep North*, by Edward Bond.

I asked him to call Fraydoon and see if I could audition for a role. The answer came quickly. I was to go to the drama workshop in two days and audition for one of the lead roles, the young British queen living in Japan.

I could not believe it and was totally skeptical. I had no theater experience and had no training except for those plays I'd put on with my cousin Nasrin. I'd performed at family gatherings and parties, entertaining an enthusiastic audience, but this was different and required at least some formal theatrical training.

Still, I had asked for it and had to do it. All of my life, I thought, I had yearned to be an actor, and this was my chance. It was a great opportunity to find out whether I had what it takes or not.

The audition took place at the workshop. I wore a summery cotton black dress with hundreds of miniature yellow birds printed on it, and a pair of dark green sandals with a wedge.

When I arrived, there were more than twenty people waiting their turn. After a while, the assistant director called my name, now Shohreh Aghdashloo, and before I knew it I was shoeless, on my knees, begging the character of Shogo, the brutal killer and revolutionary samurai who was against British colonialism in Japan, to have mercy on my children and spare them their lives.

I had memorized my lines, so I had no problem turning around freely and acting as though I were really surrounded by the enemy army in the forest with my children by my side.

Among other important people in the room was Abbas Nalbandian, a brilliant playwright, who had created his own genre of storytelling in pure Farsi, eliminating foreign words imported into the Persian vocabulary. He was the head of the workshop.

When the audition was over, I was asked to wait in the office. I was thinking I had better go home and kiss my dream good-bye, when Abbas called me to his office and said they loved the audition and were willing to hire me for seven hundred toman per month (about a hundred dollars at the time).

I was speechless. Rehearsals started in two weeks, and they were planning to put it onstage in fewer than two months.

I was remorseful on my way back home. I should have asked my husband first before making any promises. After all, we were going on our honeymoon, and I knew how excited he was about the trip. It was all mapped out and the arrangements had been made.

Aydin was already home when I arrived. He looked at me and just knew. "Why are you so worried? The honeymoon can be postponed, but you cannot postpone Edward Bond's play."

I threw myself into his arms and kissed him dearly. No one had ever understood me so well. No one before him had cared enough to see what I wanted to do with my life.

I became all ears when rehearsals started. All the actors at the workshop had to join the morning session, which consisted of workouts, physical training, and yoga. This was followed by voice-training class, where we learned how to breathe from our stomach, and how to sing. We took an hour lunch then rehearsed until four o'clock.

The actors were encouraged to do extra work at the workshop, for which they would be paid, like selling tickets at the box office, ushering the audience, and giving a hand to the lighting and sound people. Sweeping the stage was an honor, and all the actors gave an arm and a leg to do this. Sweeping was a job designed to break us away from our ego and teach us humility, to help us question our biases and feel for the people beneath us.

I was overwhelmed and exhausted by the amount of work we had to do, but I loved it. Aydin was a great support.

In the end, the play was a hit, and I received my first standing ovation. One critic wrote, "A star is born." The workshop offered me a permanent position, and I would be in many of their plays. My parents refused to see my performances, or hear me talk about them. I owed my triumph to my husband.

9

SUNRISE, SUNSET

I HAD NO experience running a household when I married Aydin, and he was very patient with me. For the first couple of weeks, we dined mostly at our favorite restaurants, depending upon our budget—Exanado and Cartier Latin. Then I took a recipe, a traditional dish of rice and chicken, from a women's magazine and prepared a meal.

It took me hours to cook the dish, and I felt like a chemist more than a chef. I prepared the table and added a few roses. I lit the candles and waited for my husband. He was so surprised when he walked in, but it didn't take long to discover that the rice was undercooked and the chicken was far from tender. I apologized profusely and offered bread and cheese instead.

Aydin laughed. "You did your best. That's what makes it precious. But you should not waste your time like this. You should read and further educate yourself. We are born to serve a purpose. Find yours. Ask your mom to find you a housekeeper like hers." And I did. Maids were affordable for the middle class, so we decided to get one for our home.

Our maid was named Mahbobeh. She was a young single mother from the slums of Tehran, with absolutely no knowledge of housekeeping. I tried to keep the secret to myself and cover for her. One day Aydin came home early and saw me doing the dishes while Mahbobeh was resting on Aydin's dark brown leather armchair, browsing through the pictures in a weekly magazine. First he laughed at me and then said, "Ask your mom to teach your servant how to cook. Or are you afraid of her?"

Eventually Mahbobeh learned how to do the household chores, and I went to work. Aydin was still at the advertising agency, but his heart was more in his paintings.

The painting that he dedicated to me and claimed to be my portrait is a portrayal of the young princess Dorothea of Denmark, originally painted by the Flemish Jan Mabuse in 1530. She holds in her hands a kind of celestial globe dictating the course of the planets. Aydin repainted it with the utmost precision, duplicating all the details in their entirety except for her face, which was sheltered in wood. I once asked him why my portrait was faceless, and he said, "Shohreh, it is because I can never tell whether you are laughing or crying."

I WAS CALLED to meet with the new director of the workshop while I was doing the last performances of *Narrow Road to the Deep North.*

He was invited to join the workshop and stage a play and

had decided on two short ones: *The Stranger* written, by August Strindberg , and *The Lady Aoi*, by Yukio Mishima.

His name was Ashurbanipal Babela (Ashur, for short). He had studied theology in Lebanon to become a priest, but his love for theater and art made him change his path and become a stage director.

Ashur had an angelic face and looked humble in his knee-length pants, faded yellow T-shirt, and a pair of flip-flops.

He wanted me to portray Mademoiselle Y and had offered Madam X to another unknown actress. I asked him to give me two weeks. After all, our honeymoon was long overdue.

AYDIN AND I took a tour to Istanbul and Beirut, the paradise of sightseers. In Istanbul our tour guide had become totally dependent on Aydin, because Aydin knew more about the sights than he did. The guide had fallen in love with a lady in her late thirties, and the two ran off on day one. My husband became the tour guide, elaborately explaining every detail, telling stories about the places we visited. I became the head of entertainment.

This meant it was my job to find the best restaurants, cabarets, and nightclubs in Istanbul, and find out what they charged per person. I collected money from those who were interested in going, then took them out to the designated club.

I'll never forget the day we visited the Topkapi Palace Museum and spent the entire afternoon trying to restore an Iranian artist's identity. There was a beautiful poem, handwritten by Mir Emad, the renowned Iranian calligrapher, displayed at the entrance of the calligraphy section at the Topkapi. But the display said that he was Turkish. Aydin was a collector of calligraphy. In fact, he had an impressive collection, which he had gathered through years of hard work. Aydin and I went to the museum's main office and asked for the supervisor. Aydin spoke Turkish and explained to the supervisor that Mir Emad was Iranian.

The supervisor replied that "Mir Emad was given amnesty by the Ottoman Empire, who lived in the Topkapi generation after generation. In fact, if they had not saved his life, he could not have created the piece. Therefore he is Turkish and not Iranian." The supervisor spoke with the utmost determination.

Aydin was furious but said nothing. Years later, he told me that the "moron" had no idea what he was talking about. "The reason Mir Emad was assassinated in Iran was because he was not given amnesty by the Ottomans," he said. "He had to return to Iran, and his enemies made the king believe that Mir Emad had converted into the Sunni sect, a branch of Islam that the Safavid dynasty did not tolerate, and the king, Shah Abbas, ordered his assassination."

Next up was Beirut, the capital of Lebanon, a city of old mansions, villas, and newly built apartment buildings, located on a peninsula next to the Mediterranean.

We walked on cream-colored sand at the beach on our first evening, watched the full moon, and had dinner in a restaurant on Ebnesinia Avenue, the popular road of restaurants and nightclubs in Beirut.

The next day, the two of us went to the gigantic temple of Baalbek, or Heliopolis. The temple is so ancient that it predates the earliest historical records. It has been restored over the centuries and has survived many empires and dynasties. It took us a few hours to get there, and to our dismay we found that it was closed due to renovations. Aydin's eyes filled with tears. He looked at the guard standing by the entrance and managed to say a few words in Arabic. The guard looked at me and smiled. He then opened the gate and let us in. I asked Aydin what he had said, and he told me, "Thou brother, I came with my beloved wife to visit this divine temple. Do not send us home empty-handed."

The two of us explored the temple and watched the incredible sunset from its highest place in peace. We were drunk on the divine beauty we had witnessed.

10

VISITING BARDOT

AFTER OUR RETURN to Tehran and a critically acclaimed performance directed by Ashur, I had promised Aydin that I would go on an exotic trip with him. The memories of our first trip with the tour made us want to travel on our own. We went to Egypt first, then Algeria.

Cairo was astonishing. The number of historic sites was overwhelming, and the nightlife was infinite. We watched an Arabic film in a magnificent cinema located in the heart of Cairo, and had dinner in a local Egyptian restaurant. We explored the pyramids and its Sphinxes. Climbing up the dark narrow stairs inside the pyramids, hunched over, was pretty claustrophobic. But being able to see the interior of the plundered tombs of Egypt's most notorious rulers, who demanded that their wealth and servants be buried alive with them, was well worth the trip.

We dined in a huge tent next to the pyramids in the Sahara known as the Sahara Cabaret Restaurant, when the full moon took over the Sahara's cobalt blue sky. The faded yellow tent was surely a couple of thousand square feet with at least a hundred seats. We were both exhausted, but the magic in the air made us stay till the end of the show and watch the mystifying finale, a group of belly dancers moving to traditional songs, bearing huge candelabras with lit candles atop their heads.

"When you are in harmony with your partner, you are in love, and the universe is on your side," my grandmother Bahar al-Sadat once told me. Her words were so true.

We went to the bazaar the next day. I had always loved visiting the old bazaar in Tehran, so I was looking forward to this one as well. Aydin wanted to see if he could find calligraphy in a cellar of an antique dealer. I wanted to get some souvenirs, including kaftans, semiprecious stones, and silk fabrics for my cushions.

We went through a couple of corridors in the bazaar, walking through the reflection of the sun in the columns of light pouring through the ceiling's openings.

A shopkeeper told us where we could find a trader who sold calligraphies, and we went to look for him. It was the exact kind of place that Aydin was looking for. There was a good amount of calligraphy inside, all reasonably priced. Aydin fell in love with two of the most expensive pieces, a beautiful piece by Mir Emad and another great one by an unknown artist. The look on Aydin's face was priceless. His eyes were shining, and he looked like a young athlete holding his first trophy.

NEXT UP WAS Algeria, another beautiful and mysterious country. We arrived in the afternoon and got to our full room around three o'clock. It was a huge room facing a valley of tall trees set against the white sky. It had dark wooden shutters, a huge chandelier delicately carved in wood, antique-looking furniture, and a vast balcony.

We started to unpack and noticed that Aydin's American edition of *Playboy* was now gone. Aydin collected the magazine, read and spoke English fluently, and always said, "Those who are opposed to *Playboy* refuse to understand that the magazine's articles are far more substantial than its young ladies."

We were wondering where we left it, and remembered that our luggage and bags were brought to our room by a shy and hairy young man. Aydin said he was not going to make a fuss about it. He decided that the young man deserved to keep the magazine more than he did. Besides, while we could buy it again, the young man could not in a million years. Not in Algeria and not in those days.

We ordered a couple of nonalcoholic drinks, and when I turned around to tip the bellhop, I was astounded by the view. The sun was setting on the horizon, and it looked humongous; its color was a golden red-orange, and it seemed as if it were setting right on our balcony. I could feel it in my throat. Its golden rays were celestial as it gracefully retired for the day.

WE DINED IN that night and made love, and went to bed early to start fresh the next day. As we set out to explore the historic sites, we were told that there were no rental cars in Algeria.

Our only choice was to negotiate with a cabdriver and have him take us to our designated sites.

We found a cabdriver, but he only spoke Arabic. Aydin did his best to tell him what we had in mind. He looked at us and smiled.

"Tourist place?" he asked.

"Yes, tourist place," we said. And he hit the gas. As we drove through the mountains, I asked Aydin if we were going in the right direction.

"Your guess is as good as mine," he said. We arrived at the beach after almost an hour. We looked at each other and got out of the cab. We had not expected to be taken to a beach.

"What is this? Why are we here?" Aydin said.

"Look, look," said the cabdriver. "Brigitte Bardot, *la maison*."

He had taken us to a posh area with grand villas to show off Brigitte Bardot's house on the beach.

We could not help but burst into laughter and finally showed him the list of the sites that we had intended to see.

WHEN WE LEFT Algeria to go home, I was thinking of the future as a sure thing, feeling happy and content, in love and being loved, and doing what I always wanted to do: acting.

At home, though, an undercurrent of rebellion was brewing.

11

FERVOR

Becoming a regular at the workshop opened my eyes to the reality of life beyond my sheltered world. A few of my fellow actors, mostly in their twenties, had already dealt with the sort of poverty that I had visited in childhood with my grandmother, and a few had already been interrogated or harassed by SAVAK, which was tirelessly looking for traitors, mostly members of the underground Communist Party who were said to have connections to Russia. My family was not bothered by SAVAK, as we had not been involved with politics since Grandfather died.

Iran was thriving. The Shah had managed to maintain an excellent relationship with America and Europe, and also to earn a fairly good reputation in Iran as a progressive leader. But his opponents thought he was megalomaniacal and an American puppet planted to convert Iran to an anti-Communist state during the cold war. Nevertheless, the Americanization of Iran had begun, and my generation was witnessing, under the Shah, the country's most glorious days. We experienced the Persian Spring, which meant Iran's transformation from a tribal and religious society into a modern society. We walked freely through the so-called truce alleys, or as my generation used to call them, the love alleys, the narrow alleys that only fit two people walking through shoulder to shoulder, holding hands, celebrating Iran's evolution. My generation was now an American generation. This was a time when love was not forbidden, and being young wasn't considered a crime, as it is today.

THE WORKSHOP LIVED up to its reputation as the most avant-garde theater. Members tended to be educated young liberals who more or less believed in true democracy. Their young and inquisitive minds did not shy away from discussing politics in public, nor were they afraid of the ramifications—until they were visited by SAVAK.

One actor was taken away for further interviews during my time there. The interrogations took place at SAVAK secret offices in a room containing only a simple desk and two chairs. Those who had experienced these sessions said that the long hours waiting in those rooms were far more terrifying than the actual period of questioning.

Ashur would not be stopped by SAVAK's threats. He had finished writing his first two plays, *Chess* and *Dolls*, by the time we returned from our vacation. Rehearsals started immediately. It was only the two of us in the plays. This time I did not have to share Ashur with other actors. I had him all to myself and learned more from him than ever before.

The themes of the plays revolved around men and women struggling to connect but ultimately unable to. Ashur and I portrayed six characters: a man and his wife, a lover and his beloved, and finally the role of parents. The conflict that Ashur was pointing out in every relationship seemed fundamental and almost impossible to resolve.

"The performances are great, but the play needs some work," one critic wrote. Another claimed that Ashur might be a "brilliant director" but he is not necessarily a "brilliant playwright."

Ashur was an intellectual and pretty fair-minded. He agreed with the critic and said, "Hear the critic out. If he is referring to something that you know is right, learn from it. Throw it in the trash can if it is wrong."

12

LOYALTY

A FRIEND OF mine, Shirin, had wanted to see me for a while, but I had been so busy at the workshop. We finally set a date, and when I opened the door to her I knew something was terribly wrong. Her big green eyes were red. Her face was puffy, her long curly blond hair was a mess, and her belly was swollen. Despite looking like she had gained weight, she seemed malnourished.

She burst into tears as she came in and explained that she was three months pregnant, out of wedlock. Her parents were extremely conservative and had no idea that she'd had a boyfriend, let alone had gotten pregnant.

"My mother would kill herself. My father would have a stroke, and my brothers would kill me. What am I going to do?" she asked me.

I felt sorry for her. I knew she was right. I asked her how she had managed to cover it up so far. She said by pretending to be ill. She said she was going to go to the Caspian to stay with her aunt, a single woman in her seventies who would understand and be able to help her.

She had tried to get an abortion, but no doctor would do it. "It is too late," she kept hearing.

I told her that she could stay with us as long as she wanted. But it was impossible. We lived in the same neighborhood as her parents, and her brothers were all over the place. They were respectable people and well known in the area.

I told her she must talk to her boyfriend. She said she did and got nowhere. He was not ready to get married and had his own problems. He was addicted to heroin, and his father, a retired general, had done his best but had to let go of him when he refused to quit for good.

Shirin's boyfriend was very handsome, somewhere between James Dean and Troy Donahue, with blue eyes. He was tall and charming and was kept alive by friends. He partied every night and crashed on different people's couches.

I told Shirin I would talk to him.

He came at lunchtime. I made him some soup, knowing he had lost four of his front teeth in a car accident. He looked pathetic and kept telling me about the gutter he lived in. He had rented a room in a slum. He said he could not take care of himself, let alone a baby. But he was willing to reconsider the marriage, if Shirin would go to the Caspian and give him time to do the right thing.

That night I asked Aydin if he would accept the child and marry my friend as his second wife. He was stunned. Sitting on the edge of the bed, he asked me twice if I really meant it, and I said, "Yes, yes, yes. It would save her life and the child."

He laughed and said he would do no such thing. I said we would keep it quiet, but he still refused.

"Do you love me? Sometimes I wonder," my husband said. "Be it quiet or not, I do not want to do this. I do not believe you. Do you know what you are getting involved with? It's dangerous."

I kissed him and whispered, "But you will do it if she gets into harm's way, won't you?"

"Let's hope she will find a way out of this," he replied.

Fortunately Shirin found her path and I did not have to share my house with a second wife. She finally told her mother the truth and went to stay with her aunt near the Caspian Sea for a while. Her boyfriend decided to marry her and would eventually take her to his parents' house, as they were willing to take care of her and their grandchild.

Aydin kept teasing me for months for being so naïve. He told our friends how I had begged him to take a second wife. Everybody laughed their hearts out. People still caught up in old traditions in Iran at this time did have two or more wives, but the modern generation thought it was archaic.

I WAS THRIVING and my career was booming. Aydin was very happy. His business was successful, too, and his collection of calligraphies was growing larger. We were attending parties and clubs during the weekends and stayed home during the week to enjoy each other's company—except for Thursdays. We decided to leave Thursday nights for our close friends. We would have them over for dinner to discuss politics, philosophy, and life over glasses of wine.

Shirin's husband, and another mutual friend of ours, the son of a famous jeweler, had invited us to my favorite nightclub, the Key Club. They wanted to thank us for taking care of Shirin.

The Key Club was private and was founded by a socialite. It was located in northern Tehran and was a hangout for the royal family. The club's regular clientele knew one another well, as did the doorman, Mr. Mohammad. He knew everybody by their full name and titles, and no one could get past him without being approved. Our hosts were running late, so we spent time talking with our other friends until they arrived.

We immersed ourselves in a nice meal, the club's specialty, called "Abgoosht"—a lamb-shank soup—while listening to the reggae band J.J. Cale. It happened to be the winter solstice and the longest night of the year, known as "Yalda," and the first night of a long weekend. Finally our hosts showed up and we stayed until one o'clock in the morning and then called for a cab home.

I will never forget the scene at our home when we got there.

As we opened the door, we could see an old lamp lying on the table, the antique embroidery gone, and the door to our bedroom wide open.

"My calligraphy collection!" Aydin cried.

We rushed to the bedroom and found it a mess. Aydin's suits and my clothes were scattered everywhere. My jewelry and his calligraphy collection were both gone.

We called the police and were told that they would send someone over in two days, when the long holiday was over. I asked them about the thief's fingerprints, and they said the fingerprints would not disappear.

"Just don't touch anything," they said.

We sat in the hallway, speechless. I looked at Aydin, and he seemed like a warrior who had lost his sword.

We called Shamim Bahar, an old friend of Aydin's. Shamim was a true thinker by any measure, and the kind of friend who would be right there to help us.

Before his arrival, I decided to sit down and write the names of our visitors, associates, and even friends—anyone who had been in our apartment—on a piece of paper.

There was no sign of forced entry. In fact, nothing was broken, and besides, what kind of a burglar knew what those handwritten pieces were?

Aydin helped me eliminate those on my list who obviously could not have committed the crime. Finally the names of our chief suspects were left on the paper.

There were two people: Shirin's husband and the son of the prominent jeweler. They were both addicted to drugs and needed the money badly. And the son of the jeweler had access to buyers who would want the collection and the jewelry.

Aydin was skeptical. He thought I had read too many Sherlock Holmes stories. But I felt certain that they had done it. We called for a cab when Shamim got there, and the three of us started the search for our suspects. I didn't know where Shirin's husband lived, but I knew very well where the other guy lived. His family's mansion was in a posh neighborhood in northern Tehran.

We told the cabdriver what had happened, and he got excited.

"So, we are now looking for the bad guy? Ha, just like in James Bond movies?" he asked.

We got to the jeweler's house at three in the morning. I asked everybody to sit in the car and wait for me. After all, I had known this guy since we were teenagers. I rang the bell a few times, and when I did not get any response I started banging on the tall, green iron doors.

Then I heard a commotion and the doors opened. My suspect stood behind his sister, shivering like a sick bird. I told him I'd rather talk to him alone, and he took me to his room.

Still shivering, he sat next to the heater. I looked at him for a while and then said, "Why? Why did you do it? Our neighbors have seen you." I bluffed. "You know my uncle is in the police department? Think of your poor father. I promise you I will not press charges against you, nor will I ever mention your name, if you tell me the truth."

He confessed: "It was Shirin's husband's idea." They had synchronized their watches to meet at a certain time and waited on the corner until we left our home. Then they got in with a key that had been copied from the one I had lent to Shirin while she was staying with us. He said he was supposed to find buyers for the stolen goods, but none of the stuff was at his place. He could not bring it home for fear his father might become suspicious.

He said he did not know where Shirin's husband lived, but we both knew he lived (for now) close to the Volkswagen showroom in downtown Tehran. He drew a map of the area, as he remembered it, and I left him alone. To say the least he was no longer my friend, and I never saw him again.

Aydin was stunned, as were Shamim and the driver. Our

next stop was the showroom. I tried to remember the night we gave Shirin's husband a ride and I had noticed a flower shop around the corner.

That was it. We drove closer to the flower shop. There was a policeman on duty outside the showroom. We told him what had happened and asked him to watch for Shirin's husband, in case he saw us and decided to run away. Then I asked the driver to park on the other side of the alley and to keep an eye on the situation. I stepped into the dark alley, hoping to find the building he lived in, and I did.

He was sheepish and started apologizing right away. He said he did not know what got into him. I told him I was willing to forget about the whole thing if he gave me my stuff back, including the key to our house. He did so right away. He gave me back everything that they had stolen, and we never pressed charges, nor mentioned their names ever again.

I got back to the cab with our belongings, and everybody was happy—except the policeman, who was hoping to arrest the guy and make a name for himself. We tipped him and got home at six-thirty in the morning. It was not only the longest night of the year but also the longest night of my life.

We slept peacefully into the next day, knowing everything was back in its rightful place.

OUR FIRST LANDLORDS had sold the complex to a man named Mr. Manafi. He was a fanatical Muslim. His wife was home most of the time but did not come to the door or show her face to strangers. She was only allowed to go out with him covered in a chador, also known as a *hijab*.

One morning Aydin was stopped by our new landlord on his way to work.

"You and your wife had a blast last night, did you not, Mr. Aghdashloo? We kept hearing all the commotions through the walls till morning and could not sleep," he said.

Aydin was deeply offended. But we had certainly grown out of our sweet little apartment and needed a bigger place. So we started shopping around, mostly in northern Tehran, where the weather was cooler and the houses were more secluded.

13

HOME SWEET HOME

AYDIN AND I moved into our own house in northern Tehran in 1974. It was a cozy three-bedroom abode with a charming front yard accentuated by a small round fountain in the middle. A huge basement and a small but lovely backyard were great bonuses.

The moment I saw the house, I knew I was going to ask Aydin to add a second floor for his mom. She was getting older, and Aydin was literally the light of her life. Living together would have made our lives easier. She would be able to be with Aydin at all times, and he would not have to make the long commute to her place every other day.

Aydin's mother, Nahid, moved into the second floor next to his atelier and extensive library, which now contained three thousand books, most of them leather bound. Mrs. Nahid, as I used to call her, was truly an angel. She was petite, very pale and skinny, with a pair of blue-green eyes, and dyed black hair. Her unique beauty and elegance made her stand out at the age of seventy-five.

Every morning she put on light makeup and a nice simple dress, as though she were going somewhere. She was kind and liberal and did not mind having me hang around in my pajamas.

Aydin was still working at the advertising agency and would come home early. He would chat with me and his mom for a while and then retire to his atelier, where he would paint and read. I loved sitting next to him sometimes, watching him paint with the utmost precision. I'd wash his brushes and observe his sorcery as he'd dissolve a small piece of gold paper in a special liquid or water and turn it into pure gold paint, which he used to give that authentic and majestic look to his icons. Aydin was an alchemist.

Living in a house required a daily housemaid, and we found a great one. Her name was Zari, and we called her Mrs. Zari. She was in her midthirties and had two young children. She was religious, wore *hijabs*, and prayed a few times a day. At six feet, she was uncommonly tall for an Iranian woman. But she was pretty, feminine, round and plump, with a pair of bright eyes that went perfectly with her smile.

She lived in the area and could walk to our house, rather than stay over. I preferred a daily helper who could cook, too. But Aydin decided to hire a real cook. His name was Hassan, a young man in his twenties, who was extremely shy and religious.

The moment Mrs. Zari walked into my life, I knew I did not

have to worry about anything. She took care of me and the house. She made sure that I ate my breakfast. She looked over my wardrobe and took care of all the cleaning and ironing. Then she would run around the house to make sure everything was in proper order.

MEANWHILE ASHUR WAS invited to stage a play at the Persepolis Art Festival in 1976, for which he wrote *Tonight, There Is Moonlight*, a seven-act play revolving around a corrupt pope and his slaves.

The stage was built in the shape of a huge cross, and the audience sat along its sides. Ashur played a tyrannical pope, taking after Velázquez's *Portrait of Pope Innocent X*, and we, the members of the workshop, played his slaves. I played the mediator, the pope's angel.

The role earned me a great review in *Plays and Players*, a prestigious magazine in the United Kingdom. A few European and American journalists and critics had traveled to the festival as well. It was the first time my work had been seen by foreigners.

TEHRAN WAS STILL under construction just as the Shah had pointed out to me years before. More old houses were demolished in favor of apartment buildings. More mansions were erected in northern Tehran, and there were thousands of high-end new cars on the roads, driving on newly built highways and renovated boulevards.

More luxurious hotels, restaurants, galleries, cinemas, and private clubs were opening; public parks were growing and so was the number of people walking through them. Aydin had introduced me to his friend Kamran and his wife, Shahla, an architect graduate. Shahla and I had a lot in common and became eternal friends overnight. With the 1973 oil crisis, the Middle East accumulated enormous wealth after OPEC increased oil prices drastically. They were getting back at the industrial powers, including the United States, to regain control of their vital commodity.

The Shah was happy to have taken a step toward the nationalization of the Iranian oil industry by joining OPEC and proud to have proven his loyalty to the United States and Europe by refusing to join OPEC in the first place. In 1974 the price of oil doubled in less than a year to $40 per barrel. (Today it costs $107 a barrel.) The Shah was never more popular in his lifetime, both inside and outside Iran.

Iranians were savoring the moment. We, too, were swept up in the current.

14

POT LADY

B Y THIS TIME my oldest brother, Shahram, was in school at the National University of Iran studying architecture. He would eventually go to Oxford to get his Ph.D. and later practice architecture in England. Shahriar, the frog dissector on the beach, was now at the National University of Iran as well, working toward a doctorate in medicine. My younger brother was not interested in a particular career. He was a straight-A student in high school and declared, "I'm just going to be an ordinary man." My mother and father were now in their late forties and finally, after a two-year embargo—my father was aghast that I had become an actor—they came to see my plays and were quite pleased by my performances.

I WAS INVITED by the "Kids of the Street" theater group, which was pretty well known for its depiction of real life on the streets of Iran, to be in one of their plays. It was headed by Ishmael Khalag, who wrote and directed his own material.

Khalag was a phenomenon. He came from the slums and learned playwriting in the slum teahouses, an aged version of today's star box, where the ill-fated men gathered to rest, chat, and smoke hookah or hand roll cigarettes. He focused on the faces of the poor and heard their stories. Khalag was very humble, despite all the great reviews he received.

He invited me to portray the lead in his play *The Pot Lady and Mash Rahim*. It had been running successfully in the workshop's repertoire for years. This was my first truly Iranian play, portraying a real woman from the gutter. It takes place in a teahouse, where a street vendor, a bricklayer, and an onion seller are the regular customers.

The Pot Lady and Mash Rahim was successfully staged at the workshop and toured the southern cities of Abadan, Ahvaz, and Isfahan. The play brought more than five thousand southerners to the theaters in nine performances.

AFTER THE PLAY, I landed my first feature film, *The Chess Game of the Wind*, playing the part of a bondmaid and directed by emerging director Mohammad Reza Aslani.

The Chess Game of the Wind is an Agatha Christie–like story of a corrupt aristocratic family murdering each other one by one, then finally by my character, a young slave. It was shot at an historic mansion that once belonged to a reputable prime minister of Iran. It was located next to Laleh-Zar, or the "tulip field," Tehran's equivalent of Broadway and a major shopping area.

It was during this production that I first met Jaleh (or Zsa Zsa), my dear friend, who would watch me prepare for the Oscars years later. She had just returned from America, where she had spent most of her young life. She was now working with Progressive Iranian Cinema, the film's production company.

Jaleh had experience working in Hollywood for a short time and followed the same methods, or rules, in producing *The Chess Game of the Wind*. She sent a car to each actor's house and made sure that every actor's demands were fulfilled. In fact, she was the one who taught us what Hollywood meant. If you pamper the actors, you get the best results. Jaleh even checked up on us at night. She wanted to make sure we did not party too late so that we would come to work fresh.

I will never forget the night I went to our hairdresser's birthday party with my costar. It was during the week, and Jaleh had somehow found out about the party and had come to send us home. We felt like teenagers with a curfew.

FOLLOWING MY WORK on *The Chess Game of the Wind* the director Abbas Kiarostami offered me the lead in his first feature film, *The Report*. He was well known for the short films he had made at the "Institute for the Intellectual Development of Children and Young Adults" (as it would be translated into English). The institute had been founded by Farah, Her Majesty the Queen of Iran. When I broke the news and told the workshop that I had another offer, they told me that if I accepted the film, I could no longer work there because I would not be available to attend on a daily basis.

I left the workshop with a lot of sorrow in my heart. I was scared of letting go and leaving my peers. After all, it had been part of my identity for several years now. I could have stayed there with a guaranteed future, but as Grandma used to say, "Even water gets stagnant, remaining in the same place for too long."

The future was unclear, but I was excited about it.

ONE AFTERNOON, WHILE considering Kiarostami's offer, I decided to take a luxurious bath, adding a couple of fresh jasmine flowers and sea salt. I turned off the light, placing two round cotton balls soaked in rosewater on my eyelids while I sat dreaming, but removed them when the door was opened and Aydin came in looking disheveled. He sat on the white and yellow tiled area, adjacent to the tub, and kept looking at me. He looked lost in the steam.

I asked him if anything was wrong, and he said he had been invited to work at Her Majesty the Queen's office as the head of the Art and Cultural Department. He was worried what his friends might think of him. When I asked him why his friends' opinions mattered to him so much, he said that there is no intellectual society in the world that could support their government. I told him that his friends might get upset with him at first but when they realized what he could do for them while holding such an important position they would understand.

The mission of the office of the queen was to preserve Iranian heritage and to promote and support contemporary Iranian arts and artists. A handful of Aydin's close friends and social acquaintances could benefit from his new position. They were extremely talented artists but not well known or privileged enough to promote their works. Aydin could indeed help.

"Even ideologues have to work within the system to survive. Take the job and help your artist friends," I said to him.

The look of worry suddenly disappeared from his face. He was smiling, as was I.

Aydin asked me what I thought about Kiarostami's screenplay. I told him that with all due respect to Kiarostami, the screenplay did not make any sense to me. He asked me what the story was about, and I said, "Nothing."

He smiled. "*Nothing* is a very important word. Why don't you read it again and see what this 'nothing' is?"

THE STORY WAS about a couple who were constantly fighting and on the verge of a nasty breakdown, due to their financial problems, even though the leading man was a tax collector.

Suddenly I felt like I had discovered a new world, just like cinema verité. I expected "drama," as in the movies I had seen previously, with twists and turns and an elongated climax. Kiarostami had instead portrayed a lower-middle-class family whose life lacked excitement and who were at the end of their rope. The real drama was the fact that there was no solution to the dilemma, where nothing can change, no miracles can happen, and no family members would ever step in.

I called Kiarostami the next day and told him I would do it.

They were not going to start shooting for another month, so I decided to go to Paris with Aydin.

Aydin had to stop in Geneva first on business. He was commissioned to buy some Iranian art and antiques that had been smuggled or stolen from Iran throughout centuries and were now being sold at prominent auction houses in Europe.

Aydin loved to shop for me, whether I was traveling with him or not. He sat for hours in French boutiques such as Yves Saint Laurent, Dior, Emanuel Ungaro, and others on the Faubourg Saint-Honoré. When he returned home, he would dress me up and I would do the catwalk for my girlfriends. They knew he had great taste and only shopped at the top designers.

In Paris together, we were walking down the Champs-Élyseés, window-shopping, and saw a crowd gathered around a pet shop window where gorgeous puppies of all different breeds were sitting and playing. There he was: a classic German shepherd, brown and gold, proudly looking at the adoring crowd. His eyes were affectionate, and he was sitting in a Sphinx position. His ears were arrogantly erect. I could not take my eyes off of him, and he was looking at me, too.

I heard Aydin whispering, "Do you want him?" I could not believe my ears. I cheered and kissed him. Aydin bought him for me and named him Pasha, meaning "sir" in Turkish. Pasha was six months old and already trained. We took him home on Iran Air the next day.

I would walk Pasha for hours in the Royal Public Park close to our house and played vigorously at home. One of our favorite activities was to dance. I'd put his paws on my shoulders, hold him tight, and we'd tango to Albinoni's *Adagio*. Aydin once said that he would never forget the sight of Pasha and me dancing.

15

THE FOUR MUSKETEERS

I STARTED WORKING on Kiarostami's *The Report* in 1976. We shot the movie in a pocket-size house, which was located close to Tehran Airport. In fact, what made the fights between the husband and wife even more intense was the constant sound of jets flying overhead.

Before we knew it, we were on our way to the Moscow Film Festival, where the film won the Critics' Choice Award and was seen by an international audience. I was finally being congratulated for my work by non-Iranians.

A WEEK AFTER my return from Moscow I received bad news about *The Report*. The film had been banned under the Shah's regime due to its premise that a tax collector's poverty would cause havoc in his family. The notion of displaying poverty was frowned upon. Despite *The Report*'s success with the critics in Moscow, it was not going to be shown in Iran.

But I could not believe it. I had heard about how bad censorship was becoming under SAVAK, which was increasing its power with the Shah, but I had not yet experienced it.

I decided to fight for the film and asked Aydin to get me an appointment (through his connections with the queen) with Mr. Pahlbod, the minister of art and culture, who was also His Majesty's son-in-law. I assumed he still had power when it came to censorship.

The ministry was located at the top of Baharestan Square. This was the same square that had witnessed many political rallies, demonstrations, and the assassination of Prime Minister Hassan-Ali Mansur, a liberal politician, on January 27, 1965. Mansur was literally a few steps away from the gates of Majlis (parliament) to deliver his first State of the Union speech, when he was shot fatally getting out of his car at Baharestan Square. He later died at a hospital. Mansur was said to have American tendencies in his politics. Four members of Fadayan Islam (martyrs of Islam) were executed in relation to his assassination.

I also have a lot of personal memories of the square. My mother used to take me to a kindergarten located right off of it every day. There was a vast round pool in the center of the square with a huge fountain in the middle of it. The fountain was lit up in different colors that kept changing while the water flowed out into the pool. I also went there with Grandmother Bahar al-Sadat to watch the ebullient festivities while enjoying cream puffs, my favorite pastry, in the hot summer evenings.

The pastry shop that sold the best cream puffs was still there. I decided to buy a couple and take them to the minister. Perhaps I was going to try to bribe him innocently with the delicacies and my charm. My appointment was at two in the afternoon, and I was right on time with my box of cream puffs. The minister's secretary asked me to wait a couple of minutes and then sent me in. The room was wide, long, and pretty dark. Its walls were covered with black-and-white pictures of the minister with the king and the rest of the cabinet as well as the minister's diplomas and other assorted decorations. The minister was sitting behind his magnificent desk at the rear of the room next to a large window with half-open blinds.

I walked in and shouted my hello, loudly and awkwardly. But as I took literally my second step toward him, I lost my balance and hit the chair next to his desk. Luckily, I managed to hold on to the box of cream puffs and offered them as soon as I landed near his desk.

I could see he was dying to laugh at me but was also impressed by my courage. After all, I had the audacity to make an appointment with him and complain about censorship in Iran. He listened carefully to my issues and said nothing. At the end he promised that he would personally look into it and do his best to release the film.

The film was never released.

AYDIN WAS CONSTANTLY traveling in search of Iranian treasures, yet he still managed to exhibit his paintings at the spacious gallery at the Iran-America Society for two weeks. The gallery's theme during that time was the face of Botticelli. Aydin had several paintings that were interpretations of the master's. The exhibition was extraordinary and so was the turnout. Art lovers, collectors, connoisseurs, students, along with ordinary people visited. Everyone loved Aydin's work.

ALTHOUGH *THE REPORT* did not find its way to the silver screen in Iran, I was receiving offers from filmmakers who had managed to see it. One script, *Broken Hearts*, came to me, and I fell in love with the tragic love story of a prostitute and her mentally disordered lover. It was written by the Iranian screenwriter Ali Hatami, who died of cancer in 1996. He was also slated to direct the film and had offered me the role of the prostitute, playing opposite Behrooz Vossoughi, Iran's superstar actor and the equivalent of a dark-haired Steve McQueen.

Broken Hearts was shot mostly in a traditional house south of Tehran in the winter. It turned out to be one of the classics of Iranian cinema and garnered me the fame in Iranian films to which I owe my career. I literally gave away two months of my life and focused on portraying this character with the utmost naturalness, actively trying to shed any theatrical mannerisms or clichés.

I LEFT TEHRAN soon after the shooting was done and went to Rome with Aydin and our best friends, Behnam and his wife, Dokhi. Behnam was a genius. He was a critic, hosted his own TV show on the Iranian national network at the age of twenty-four, and spoke high Farsi and fluent English. He was certainly a man with no patience for mediocrity. He was thin and dark, with an uncanny resemblance to Einstein, including the same wild hairstyle.

Dokhi on the other hand was an introvert and calm at all times. She was an intelligent, petite young woman with an incredible view of the world. She had studied psychology in Iran and France, and at twenty-four was already working part-time at a psychiatric hospital in northern Tehran.

I had gotten to know them at the workshop. They had come to see one of my plays and waited to see me when it was over. Soon I found out that Behnam was the critic who, after seeing my first work, suggested: "A star is born." I invited them to our place, and it was the beginning of what seemed like an eternal friendship. Dokhi and I became friends immediately and were inseparable. Although Aydin was more than ten years older than Behnam, they had a lot in common. Aydin had a tremendous respect for both of them and for what they had achieved at such young ages. We became the four musketeers and traveled together.

16

MA NON È UNA COSA SERIA

WHEN WE GOT home, Behnam had decided to put together a play and form a private-sector theater that had no affiliation with the government. He started raising the money from his father, as well as a couple of his father's friends.

He then chose the director, Iraj Anvar, a prominent and renowned Iranian stage director. Anvar suggested that we should stage a popular and meaningful light comedy like *Ma non è una cosa seria*, meaning "the concept is not serious," by Luigi Pirandello, the Italian dramatist and novelist, who received the Nobel Prize in literature in 1934. The play revolved around a Casanova, his entourage, and an unattractive innkeeper. The success of *Broken Hearts* had convinced Behnam to ask Behrooz Vossoughi to portray Casanova to my unattractive innkeeper.

We first asked the City Theatre, the hub of avant-garde playwrights and directors, to let us launch the play there. But

we were told after a couple of days of rehearsals that the theater's artistic committee had decided that they would not accommodate us because our play was more commercially
driven than artistically motivated, the movie stars in the play
made it even more commercial, and the ticket price suggested
by Behnam was going to exceed that of the other plays staged
there.

Part of the play's purpose was to create a new generation of
theatergoers by attracting passersby, young adults, and movie
buffs who'd like to see their movie stars on the stage at the City
Theatre, conveniently located at a beautiful park at the heart of
Tehran. Our next and best choice was the Iran-America Society. We did eighty consecutive performances at the Iran-
America Society. One included a private performance for the
charity organization of the Shah's sister, Princess Ashraf. Those
Iranians who believed that dictatorship was the only way to
keep the country under control also believed that Princess
Ashraf would have been a stronger candidate to run the coun-
try than her brother.

Princess Ashraf came to see the play with an army of generals and their wives. During intermission, we found out that she
had decided to dine at the theater, and her cook had sent a
couple of trays of rice and cherries with saffron chicken from
the palace. A huge dining table was erected in the middle of the
Iran-America Society's inner courtyard, and we had to wait for
an hour and a half for her and her guests to finish their dinner.
Finally, when we were about to go onstage to start the second
half, we received another request from the generals: they were
wondering if we could make the second half shorter, so they

could make it home in time to watch the Iranian and Israeli soccer match.

I was angry and offended. I went to the director and told him, "We cannot do this." We finished our entire production— and they loved it. The princess came backstage and greeted us, saying, "This is the best play I've ever seen."

17

THE DREAM OF SULTANIEH

I WAS GOING through the final stages of what would be my last film in Iran, *The Mirage of Sultanieh*, when the turmoil began. Politics had been shifting toward a more conservative viewpoint on how Iran should be run. The Shah had lost control of the majority of the country. The irony of the film was in its excruciating resemblance to the country's affairs at the time. The film was a contemporary portrayal of an architect and his nightmares of an attack on Iran's soil by the Mughal Empire while restoring a medieval mosque on the outskirts of an old city. In his dreams he sees himself back in medieval times facing hundreds of Mughal soldiers on horseback who attack Iran and slaughter innocent Iranians, with their swords shining in the air.

I still vividly remember the last time I saw Parvin Ansari,

the director of the film, at the dubbing session. We were both shaken by the chilly winter and the chaos that was now arising on the streets, where young people were setting tires on fire.

Neither one of us knew that we would never see each other again, or that we'd never see the finished film, which we hoped would be released outside the country—my first for Iranians living abroad. Ideally, it would have been dubbed for English-speaking audiences as well. My last Iranian film was simply lost in the anarchy that brought the Islamic Republic to power.

I still remember watching the BBC newsreel a little after Ayatollah Khomeini had come to power. Excited mobs had taken over the House of Cinema, the archive of classic and con-temporary Iranian films. They were violently emptying the shelves, the vaults, the silver cans, throwing their contents out the windows, holding on to the tips of the films and rolling them down the building.

Just like in any other underdeveloped country, when a leader is deposed, killed, or sent into exile, all the elements of his rule are banished from the face of the earth according to those now in charge, regardless of their historic or sentimental value.

In all likelihood, our film had shared the same fate while mobs wreaked havoc in the fall of 1978.

PARVIN CALLED ME a couple of years later when I was in London, and asked me if I could help her find the film. I called my friends in Iran and told them that Parvin was willing to pay up to $50,000 for a copy of the film. My sources did their best to find one, exhausting every avenue, but it was nowhere to be found. I still remember the night my friend called from Iran and told me the film must have been destroyed. What had happened to my country? What injustices had these people faced to make them so ignorant and so angry? Why did they have to act like barbarians, destroying art? Who are these people? They certainly do not look like Iranians to me.

18

THE NIGHTS OF
THE REVOLUTION

T EHRAN IS IN chaos. The city's traffic is paralyzed by daily demonstrations. Painted signs read DOWN WITH THE SHAH. The Ayatollah Khomeini's audiotape is playing on every cassette player in Tehran. His voice is firm and demanding, even though he is in exile in France. He is blaming the Pahlavi dynasty for all the Western influence and corruption in Iran. Religious fanatics are getting behind him.

"Look closely at the map of Iran. Look at all the yellow, red, blue, and other colorful dots on it. Look closely. They are not just dots on the map. They are the colors of Iran's great resources: oil, uranium, copper, turquoise, and many more. All these belong to you, the people of Iran, not to Pahlavi's dynasty. Demand your rights," says the Ayatollah.

Overwhelmed by Ayatollah Khomeini's accusations and

promises from exile, the whole country is now shifting from left to right by the hour.

Iran is suffering from an exhilarating prerevolutionary mood. First there were the demonstrations, then massive rallies followed by rounds of strikes. The fear of a general strike lurks.

Angry crowds chanting slogans have now turned into rioters demanding the Shah's abdication. Tehran is shrouded in tear gas and smoke. The Shah's picture, once mandatory in government offices, is flying out of every office building in Tehran into the abyss.

There is fire everywhere. Our city is painted the color of orange and red. Mobs are burning more and more stolen tires, and the Shah's pictures are discarded in piles on the streets.

I hear the news on the radio that Pahlavi Boulevard, where my best friend lives, is aflame and I jump into action.

Getting close to her apartment building via car is impossible, so I ask Saeed, my driver, to circle around and meet me on the other side of the alley. People are running and shouting in the thick black smoke. When I get to Shahla's apartment, I find her standing in the middle of the hallway, next to her scared Indonesian maid. Her four-year-old son, Ali, tries to shove as many miniature toy cars into his pockets as possible.

I ask Shahla to go with me. But she is worried. She cannot let go of her home. "Take Ali and the maid with you. I can't leave," she says to me.

The police come to tell us that we have to evacuate the building. We all get out, and I leave with Ali in my arms and the maid running behind me, looking for my driver. I'll never forget Shahla's worried face as she stood on the opposite side of the main street looking at her apartment, waiting for it to burn down.

OUR THURSDAY-NIGHT GET-TOGETHERS had now turned into every other night. Friends came over, and we met in our tearoom, facing the front yard and its tall walls. The turmoil had gotten worse. We were all worried, not knowing what the future had in store for us.

One of our regular guests was "Mr. S.," a clever guy in his late twenties, a critic and a writer. Another was Mahdi, my family friend and one of Aydin's best friends. Mahdi was suspicious of Mr. S. He believed that Mr. S. was visiting a powerful religious leader named Talaghani before he joined us. Talaghani was said to have had some connections with the Communists. Mahdi believed that the Communist Party was helping the clerics get rid of the Shah, in hopes of eventually turning Iran into a Communist country.

Another friend of ours was Ali, whom we called Professor Ali for his endless knowledge in every field, especially in philosophy. Professor Ali believed the collusion between the clerics and the leftists may have been true, but it would be the clerics who would get rid of the leftists.

The rest of our friends joined us one by one during those revolutionary nights in Tehran. Among them was another of my closest friends, Margan. She was a petite beauty with a short, shiny black bob, and emerald green eyes. She and I checked after friends in different neighborhoods even after the curfew was passed. Margan had a Mini Minor, a British car, which we could drive through even the tiniest alleys in Tehran.

By the imposed martial law, everyone had to go home before nine o'clock in the evening, except for emergencies. But our gatherings started at nine o'clock, and we made up stories to tell the authorities if we ever got busted, such as "I'm visiting my father on his deathbed."

Wherever we went, or whomever we visited, we could smell the fear, the fear of the unknown, the fear of losing one another and our country. The uncertainty filled the air, and nobody could trust anybody. The lights on the streets were turned off after nine o'clock, and power shortages added to the creepiness of the dark nights.

We kept having meetings and discussing politics in the candlelight, behind closed curtains, listening fearfully to the most popular slogan of the time, "Allah Akbar"—meaning "God is great"—from nearly every rooftop night after night.

I was visiting my colleagues and friends at the theater workshop where I started acting when I heard the Shah's last speech on Iranian national radio. He urged Iranians to open their eyes and not to fall into the trap of fundamentalism. He promised everyone that he would do his best if his people stood by him. We all looked at one another, wanting to believe that everything would get back to normal under his power. But a thick cloud of doubt hung over our heads.

In a few weeks, the Shah left with tear gas in the air. This was January 1979. I will never forget his last gesture. He bent down and collected a bit of Iran's soil before he flew off in his plane. He looked much older than his age. His eyes were filled with tears and disappointment. He was suffering from cancer, though none of us knew about it. It was truly heart-wrenching.

The rioters, mostly young men, were holding up enlarged

copies of the morning headlines, stating in big black letters, THE
SHAH HAS FLED IRAN. Students chanted in unison, "Allah Akbar,
Khomeini Rahbar" ("God is great, Khomeini is our leader").
They were soon joined by the leftists, socialists, Communists,
Islamic Marxists—and even the rightists. In my heart I still
loved the Shah, but witnessing the hatred and dissatisfaction of
hundreds of thousands of Iranians marching on the streets, demanding the Shah's abdication, was telling me that perhaps
Iran was ready for a change, under someone who came from
the people, and worked for the people. Could it truly be the end
of the Shah's dynasty? Has he really left for good? Will he ever
return? People kept asking one another the same questions.
The speculations were endless. Some believed that he would
soon regain power with the help of the CIA, as he had in August
1953, claiming, "History repeats itself."

The overall picture was as macabre as reading *The Trial* by
Franz Kafka. Only this time, a kingdom was on trial by its own
youth, demanding the king abdicate and for Khomeini to
return. They naively believed that Khomeini was going to be
their Gandhi—which time and history would prove wrong.

The Shah had left the country to Prime Minister Shapour
Bakhtiar, the last prime minister of Iran and one of the most
distinguished. Still, the rumor was that the Ayatollah was returning to Iran via Air France.

Prime Minister Bakhtiar called for a peaceful pro-Shah demonstration at Baharestan Square, the same square where I had
gone to see the minister with my puff pastries. My father asked
me to stay away from the demonstrations, knowing I had been
out at every chance. I had begun doing so ever since the Shah

had left because I was curious to see what a revolution was all about. And here I was, now a part of it.

My father knew me well and was genuinely afraid for me. He kept saying that he was more afraid of what I might do than of what my three brothers might do. Aydin, too, wanted me to stay away from the streets and the rioters. But history was unfolding before my eyes. Witnessing people en masse, marching on the streets, putting their lives in danger, to make a change, was electrifying. I felt I was in the midst of collective minds and a kind of oneness and a civil disobedience that bore all the ingredients of a Shakespearean tragedy.

I heard them out but ultimately carried on with my actions, because I found it so meaningful and exciting. I truly believed in the monarchy and thought it was the best form of government, at least for Iran, so I screamed my opinions out loud with the rest.

ONE DAY I left home with Mahdi a little after Aydin had gone to work and headed toward the crowds. Aydin worked tirelessly until the last days of the Shah's reign, and when the queen's office was shut down, he decided to work on his own as an artist. Saeed, our driver, ran after Mahdi and me and asked why we had not taken the car. We told him that we were going to see a friend in the neighborhood and did not need it. We then walked to Tajrish Square and tried to catch a cab. No driver wanted to go anywhere near the demonstration. We paid one cabdriver a lot of money to take us as close as he could. Still, it took us half an hour on foot to get to the demonstration, through the alleys of my childhood neighborhood.

Thousands of pro-Shah Iranians, men and women dressed up for the occasion, walked miles on Shah Avenue for Baharestan Square. There were others, mostly bearded men and women in *hijabs*, all dressed in black shouting, "Allah Akbar, Khomeini Rahbar," as they angrily shook their fists at us.

A line of masked policemen, armed to the teeth, holding on to their see-through shields along the edge of the pavements, protected the peaceful demonstrators—like us—from the fanatics, who were growing more and more hostile.

We joined the peaceful demonstrators but with difficulty, having to cut through both the angry demonstrators and the chain of armed policemen.

The crowd took us to the square and Prime Minister Bakhtiar appeared. People cheered, many booed, but all soon quieted down, waiting for him to speak.

He started with a poem by Hafiz: "God be with the one—who has traveled with caravans of our love. . . ."

He paused before the second verse, and somebody screamed, "He means God be with the bloody Shah, you idiots." The crowds started shoving and pushing. Some shouted "Death to the Shah and the filthy monarchists" while others were screaming and crying. Then somebody threw the first brick, which was soon followed by hundreds of them. The scene was like a raging coliseum, only this time it was brother against brother.

A half-broken brick hit me on the forehead. Mahdi rushed me to the nearest road-going emergency ambulance, where I was lucky to receive only eleven stitches.

I got home late that evening and Aydin was on the verge of a nervous breakdown. "Shohreh," he said. "You must stay home away from the trouble, or leave Iran."

I was shocked at his suggestion. I had never thought about leaving Iran for political reasons. How long would I have to leave for? I wondered.

BAKHTIAR NEEDED TO make a vital decision: whether or not to have the Ayatollah arrested upon his arrival for his anti-Shah propaganda.

He ordered all the airports shut down for three days, or possibly more, perhaps to buy time to find a popular solution for this divided nation.

Poor Bakhtiar was never forgiven by Khomeini for shutting down the airports. He eventually fled the country but was stabbed to death in 1991 in his own house in Paris, under the nose of the French police. Bakhtiar's assassins were said to be of Iranian origin and reportedly escaped back to Iran via Switzerland.

19

THE BOXES OF MY LIFE

I SAT IN our backyard for hours, weighing my options. I considered the consequences if I chose to leave. I would be far from my husband, family, and friends at least for a while and waiting to see what the future had in store for me. I needed to leave Iran, even though the idea broke my heart. I was too much of a danger to my family and my husband. I had no intention of putting members of my family in danger by attending the demonstrations. I had no idea if my film work or my political beliefs were going to haunt me in the new regime.

The chaos and the slogans that littered the streets disturbed me greatly. For endless empty days I was upset not only at the distrust among the people but also about the question of what I could even do in my country if I remained. After all, I was no longer acting, just watching Aydin paint and listening to my mother-in-law's fearful view of the outcome of the revolution.

Parting with three-year-old Pasha was also a devastating thought. I could not take him with me. I did not even know where I was going. My instinct was telling me to leave. My destination was as unknown as my future.

Aydin came home one night and saw me sitting in the dark with Pasha, listening to Albinoni's *Adagio*, the sad classical music permeating our home. He got very upset and told me then and there, "You are free as a bird to do what is right for you. I will help you leave. I will do anything for you to be happy again and live a life that you deserve. I know that I cannot keep you here, and I know that I cannot live abroad. But I am not telling you what to do, or what not to do. You are free to make the decision, and I will support you as long as I am alive. I will be behind you like a mountain."

I prepared to leave Iran with a small suitcase containing a few pieces of clothing, including two of my favorite theater costumes, five photographs of my family, and the iconic portrait that Aydin had painted of me on my twenty-second birthday. Last but not least, I packed the two calligraphies we'd purchased in Egypt.

I left after two months of intense deliberations. The idea of leaving all the people I loved was killing me, and starting a new life seemed difficult and daunting. But I had no other choice. What could a young, modern, outspoken actress do under the Islamic revolutionary regime that was about to take over?

We had a small Persian dresser from around 1800 with many drawers. It was known as "Hezar Bisheh," or "1,000 nests." In one of the drawers were two small dictionaries. One was English-Farsi, the other Farsi-English. I opened one and started looking at the English words. I tried to pronounce big words, such as *psy-chi-a-trist* or *squan-de-ring*. Pasha looked at me in the way a wise man looks at his idiot pupil.

I knew that my little knowledge of the English language would not take me far, and I wondered if I could easily learn the rest of the language shortly—naively believing it possible.

PROFESSOR ALI WAS right. The clerics eventually wiped out most of the underground leftists who did not or could not flee the country. The Shah moved to Cairo with his family to stay with his friend Anwar Sadat.

I called my childhood friend Mahdi and told him that I had to leave the country and by car. It was the only way left to sneak out of the turmoil. He laughed at me: "You're crazy, but I'm crazier than you. I'll help you get out, but I will return to Iran after you are settled. I cannot live anywhere but here."

Next I called my mother. Our conversation was brief.

"Mom, I am leaving," I said.

"When?" she asked

"Tonight," I replied.

"You know how much I love you, Shohreh. Do what is right for you. And remember, your father and I are proud of you, wherever you are."

"I love you, too, Mom."

"God be with you," she said.

"May I talk to Dad?" I asked.

"It would be better if you didn't," my mother told me. "I'll tell him and your other two brothers later."

She knew me. She knew that if I had stayed I would have put

everybody's life in danger, including my own. I was too outspoken, daring, and idealistic for the Islamic regime that was determined to take Iran back into medieval times.

Next I called my brother Shahriar, who was now married and living in his own house. He came right over. I told him that I had to see my best friend, Shahla, but that I was afraid to drive alone. Shahriar and I arrived at Shahla's house a little after eight o'clock in the evening. We worried whether we would be able to make it home by the nine-o'-clock curfew.

Shahla was stunned to see me. She could not believe I was leaving Iran, but she was happy for me. We hugged and silently wept in each other's arms, and I left without saying good-bye. My last words were "See you soon, Shahla."

Thankfully we made it home on time. Mahdi had arrived and Aydin's mother was shocked to see us leaving. Aydin had decided to give her the news of our departure at the last minute and was now trying to convince his mother that he would be back in no time. The poor lady didn't understand the meaning of it all. "But why are you doing this?" she kept asking.

"Believe me, Mom, it's best for everybody," he said.

She turned to me and asked, "Do you not love Aydin?"

I was stunned. "Yes, I do love him. That is why I am doing this. I don't want him to get into trouble over me."

I SAT ON the stairs of the front yard with Pasha at my side, looking at the fountain and its translucent water in the cold. The moon and stars were shining against the dark night sky. All the flower bushes were buried under layers of thick ice. Not a sound was heard from the alley, and not a soul passed by. I couldn't even hear the wailing echo of winter crows. I sat there in total despair, preserving all the good memories of my dream life in Iran.

We ate a small late dinner while discussing which road we would travel.

We prepared to leave at four-thirty in the morning. Pasha was anxiously waiting at the door, in between my mother-in law and Hassan. Pasha was a true companion, full of love and affection, and I could tell he fully understood what was going on. His ears were erect, and I knew he sensed this was our good-bye.

I sat face-to-face with Pasha in his favorite Sphinx position, looked him in the eye, and talked to him. He listened with the utmost patience. Once I told him that I had to go, his eyebrows rolled down and his eyes became wet with sorrow. I kissed his forehead and hugged him good-bye.

At 4:30 A.M., on February 28, 1979, I left Iran. Like thousands of other Iranians departing the country every day, I, too, thought that I would return after the turmoil had ceased, possibly in only a few weeks. Surely I'd be home again.

20

BORDER PATROL

MAHDI KEPT ADVISING me to hide my jewels while leaving Iran. "Keep them underneath the car or beneath the backseat while going through the border," he said. He told me that if they were found I would go to jail for smuggling my own jewelry, which included some very valuable pieces handed down to me from my mother and other gifts from my husband.

Mahdi was right. No one was allowed to take any kind of valuable items outside the country without declaring it at the border. They were considered national heritage and were not permitted to leave the country. And those who did not obey the law had their valuables confiscated by armed guards at the border and were often jailed.

A prominent doctor and his wife had been busted. She had hidden her seven-carat diamond wedding ring in her bra. After

being thoroughly searched by two female police, who found
the ring, she was told that the diamond was an Iranian treasure
and belonged to the people of Iran. She had to turn it in before
leaving.

"You idiots," she screamed. "The real treasure is my husband, a great doctor who is leaving you! Here, take it." She then
tossed the ring into the air.

I had no intention of hiding my jewels. My instinct told me
to place the bag in an obvious place: the glove compartment. I
assumed I would not be punished for not mentioning the jewels
if they were not hidden.

WE DROVE THIRTY miles per hour along treacherous roads. It
took Mahdi, Aydin, and me days to reach the border with
Turkey. The revolution had spread to the small towns and tiny
villages. We slept in various hotels to avoid the curfew.

The scene at the border was chaotic. There were thousands
of cars, bumper to bumper, filled with Iranians claiming they
were going to Turkey for a short visit.

We arrived at the checkpoint before sunset. The border officers had us stand by the car while they searched it thoroughly.
The first place they looked was indeed underneath the car. The
second was the backseat and under the front seats, and then the
trunk. They looked at every corner, inch by inch. My heart was
going to stop. I could have never imagined that one day I would
be in danger for stealing my own jewelry.

After some time, they finally left the car and ordered us to
drive off. At last we were free to leave. We sat straight in the car
and drove away slowly, stunned by the fact that no one, absolutely no one, had paid any attention to the glove compartment.

The sun was setting and the road was icy. Mahdi was driving, with Aydin next to him in the front seat. I sat in the back to look at my birth country through the rear window as I left it behind.

That is my Persia, I thought, the land of great poets and philosophers such as Omar Khayyam, Firdawsi, and Rumi. It was the land of one thousand and one nights. The moon would remain forever that blue.

Farewell, I said to myself.

ONCE IN TURKEY, all I could think of was that I was being given the chance of living in peace again. Freedom and democracy were the only ideas that could distract me from crying as we drove down Turkey's snowy roads.

It was hard to figure out what our immediate future had in store for us. But we had seen what was happening in Iran. I had no intention of hiding who I was or losing my career as an actress. I could not afford to wait. And I happened to be right.

Well-known female and male actors who stayed in Iran and had to obey the revolutionary government were mostly interrogated and banned from acting for the rest of their lives. They were considered to be *taghoti*, or "the filthy rich." Some elderly actors were later pardoned by the regime and some managed to appear in small roles in Iranian films after twenty or more years. A couple of them died young, of heart attacks or brain strokes, having lost their hope and zest for life. When there is no hope there is no life. A few left Iran eventually, of which only a handful became successful abroad.

I remember arriving in Istanbul on a cold sunny day. The Iranian revolution had had a tremendous effect on Turkey. The

Turkish government, too, had imposed a curfew, so we could drive only during the day and again stayed at random hotels at night. Our plan was to go to London, where I could stay with my aunt, by way of Yugoslavia and Germany.

We left Istanbul two days later and started heading toward Yugoslavia, but Mahdi could no longer drive. He was extremely sick with a kidney infection and could not sit up straight. I had to drive—since Aydin didn't—and I found it funny that I had hardly driven in the city, let alone on country roads, and now I had to drive this strange international route. I did not even know how to park a car, yet I was driving one.

No matter how much I loved adventure, I was tired and homesick when we arrived in Yugoslavia. I was still praying that the Shah would return soon so we could make a U-turn and go home. But I had no choice but to move ahead, something I have never forgotten since I left my birth country.

SINCE MAHDI WAS not feeling well, we decided to rest for two days in Yugoslavia. Our original plan was to go to Germany next, but Germany had officially announced that it now required visas for Iranians. Until then, none of the European countries had required visas for Iranians. Now the only way to get to England was to go through Italy and France, before they, too, required visas for us. The European governments were re-evaluating their relationships with Iran by the minute while also trying to maintain a profitable oil connection with the revolutionary government.

We were on the road before we knew it. Mahdi was lying on the backseat again, I was driving, and Aydin was reading the map. We managed to get ourselves to Italy and decided that, no matter what, we would visit Venice. We knew that it might be our final chance to spend a few days together, and we could also let Mahdi rest.

Venice exuded love. Two days there was a luxury. It was like taking a break in the middle of a hurricane. For the first time in a couple of months, I was feeling safe and sane again. The three of us were enjoying a certain kind of happiness that does not come about until you've experienced the worst.

Having observed and absorbed the beauty of ordinary life once again made us realize how one takes life for granted in a peaceful and seminormal environment.

Aydin told me years later that he would never forget the eve of our arrival in Venice: "We were looking for a hotel. You were walking ahead of us in your long Russian fox coat. You had your backpack on, and your long brown curly hair was scattered over your shoulders. 'Look at her,' I said to Mahdi. 'Is she not a combination of all the contradictions?' Mahdi smiled, you disappeared in the fog, people were calling each other in the fog and all I could hear was an Italian man calling to his friend, 'Alberto, Alberto. . . .'"

MAHDI WAS BEGINNING to feel better, and we had to keep going, heading south to France. Though we were dying to know what was happening back home, there was still no news coming out of Iran. We did not have access to a television, nor did we speak French. The Ayatollah had shut down communication with the outside world, and foreign reporters were not welcome.

The French-Italian border was in chaos due to the high number of tourists traveling through it. It took hours to get to the checkpoint. The French officers did a thorough search and asked us to step into their office. It turned out that they were suspicious of the painting that Aydin had done of me. They actually thought it was a real iconic painting being smuggled into France with its face covered in wood. We had waited several hours for it to be examined by their experts before we were released.

We stayed a night in Nice, in the south of France, in a typical bed-and-breakfast, which looked like a miniature watchtower, in a semiround and narrow three-story building with spiral staircases, facing the ocean.

Next up was Paris. We arrived early in the morning, and the first thing we did was park our car on the Champs-Élysées and go to a movie, *Superman*, in a movie theater that was once bombed by the terrorist Carlos.

After the movie we realized that our car was gone. We told the local police and found out that our car had been towed. We decided to pick it up on our way to London the next day, knowing we would face the same problem again if we were to drive the car around town.

We checked into a nice hotel we knew of in Saint-Germain-des-Prés. Aydin told me in private that Mahdi wanted to visit Pigalle, a tourist district with lots of sex shops and prostitutes on the side streets, but he needed Aydin to translate for him. I was not supposed to know.

They left, and I took a walk and eventually met Aydin and a couple of our friends, now expatriates, at our favorite place, Café de Flore, around the corner from our hotel.

Everybody was skeptical. They believed that whatever was happening in Iran was not going to end soon. One friend suggested I stay in Paris. I told him I preferred to live in London; I had traveled to London a couple of times and was familiar with its culture. Besides, my aunt lived part-time in London and I was hoping to stay with her first and then find a place of my own.

The next day we hopped a cab to the tow pound. We showed our passports and received a ticket, which we paid in cash.

"Where are you from?" asked the policeman, who had read the morning news.

"We are from Iran," said Aydin.

"Poohhh, Iran terminé" ("Iran is finished"), said the police officer. We looked at each other in disbelief. Just what did he mean? We learned the army had at last joined the revolutionary government by announcing its loyalty to the Islamic revolution.

Up until then, our only hope was that the army would remain independent. It was obvious which side the country was shifting to, namely Muslim fundamentalism with the Ayatollah Khomeini as the supreme leader of Iran.

None of us felt like talking. The turning point of our lives had arrived and we had entered a new era.

Mahdi once asked me what I would do if I could not get financial help from my parents or Aydin. I said, "I would wash dishes, but I would be free when I am washing dishes and waiting on tables, or taking orders from hungry customers."

We left Paris knowing the bridges that connected us to the past were falling one by one. Mahdi was worried he and Aydin might get into trouble when they went back. He was pacing back and forth, speculating about what might happen.

Aydin was quiet, but I could see he was worried, too. "I have lived a clean life and have done a lot for my country. Nobody can deny that. I love my country, and I am going back to it," he said.

I felt bad for putting Aydin in such a horrible position. But it was too late. We were already in Calais, about to embark on a gigantic ship that would take us and my car to England.

We arrived in London in the early afternoon, and it was dark already.

We got ourselves a nice room, close to where my aunt lived. I called her early the next day, but she did not answer. My mother had told me that my aunt was going to London a few days before I left Iran. She should have been in London by now, unless something had kept her back.

I did not want to call my parents and put them and my brothers in harm's way or have them worry about me. I had no clue what was happening to them but did not want to add to their misery.

Finally I phoned a friend I had met in London on my first trip to England with my mother back in 1971, when we vacationed and shopped. I asked his advice on finding a good place for me to stay. Ian, a young gentleman in his late twenties, had a great sense of humor and loved Woody Allen as much as I did. He had visited Iran right before the revolution and had to return to London when the turmoil started.

He gladly offered me a place to stay on the top floor of his house. It was a large room with a view of Fulham Road at the heart of London, in a charming three-story house on a street full of idyllic town houses. I did not know what to say. His generosity made me feel like crying. He became upset when Aydin mentioned renting the room and insisted there would be no charge.

I strongly believed I would be able to take care of myself, at least for a while, until things got back to normal.

AYDIN AND MAHDI left after four days. Aydin and I kissed each other in a way that was similar to when I kissed him on his way to the office, pretending we would see each other soon, though our hearts were telling us we may not be able to see each other for a while. I had done my best to convince him and Mahdi to stay longer. Aydin was a great painter and also a great restorer, especially of calligraphy, and could find a good job in London. But Aydin was as determined to go back as I was determined to move ahead. They left and flew back to Iran; the airport was once again open.

21

ANOTHER COUNTRY

WHEN IAN WENT to work at his father's sports club, I took his dog, Fuchsia, for a walk in Fulham. I had been feeling strange, lonely, and empty. It was a certain kind of emptiness that I had never experienced before. I had never felt so lonely before in my life. I was used to being swallowed by love and companionship, and now I was alone.

Who am I? What am I doing here? I should be walking my dog now. Where is Pasha? I tried to push all the negative thoughts away and think only of good ones. I dreamed of the day when I could speak English fluently. I felt reborn in an entirely new environment, where people could take their dogs to the park and men and women could walk hand in hand, discussing love or politics.

But no matter how hard I tried, my face was wet with tears when I returned home. Ian was preparing dinner for his girlfriend, Susan, and his friend Robert. He thanked me for taking Fuchsia for a walk and asked me why I was crying. All I said was, "Why me?"

Ian replied, "I never thought that you would let go of your career, your husband, your beloved family, your dog, or your lavish life. Now that you have, you might as well make use of it rather than pitying yourself. Self-pity is the worst thing a person can do to herself."

There are times in life when we need true friends to tell us the truth, to make us snap out of it, no matter how bitter the truth is. Ian was right. I should have realized that I was not different from the rest of the people of the world. What had happened to me had happened to millions of displaced people who simply had refused to conform and had to leave their homes.

ON MY FIRST weekend, Ian was visiting his parents in Denham, and took me along. They lived in a mansion in the Buckinghamshire suburb. His parents and sisters were so nice and compassionate. His father asked me a couple of questions regarding the politics of Iran, and I got tired of struggling to make sense of the political situation in Iran with my little knowledge of English.

His mother took me to their garden and cut roses with her delicate hands covered in white cotton gloves. I carried her basket for her, and she laid the roses in a row in the basket while telling me about her life in the suburbs. They also had a house in London next to their sports club, but she preferred to live in Denham.

Spending two days in a family atmosphere was blissful, and I was so thankful to them for having me and making me feel at home. They even let me cook a Persian meal.

Aydin called on the following Monday. They had arrived safely home via Iran Air. We talked about the family, his mother, and Pasha but did not say a word about Iranian politics in case someone was listening. He begged me to call him immediately if anything went wrong or if I needed anything.

Ian's mother told me that the Berlitz School was well known for teaching English to foreign students in a short time, so I went there the next day. Fortunately it was not very expensive and I could start right away. I was back to school again, only part-time. The small dictionaries that I had brought with me became an important part of my life.

Aydin kept calling and asking if I needed anything, and I told him I was still fine. My last bit of cash was going quickly, but I did not say a word about this to Aydin and assured him that I still had enough money. I knew I was going to sell my car and jewelry to start, but kept postponing it, as though I were waiting for someone else to make the decision for me.

During my second week at Berlitz, I went to an Iranian news store on Kensington High Street to search for larger dictionaries and was devastated by what I saw on the front page of Iran's *Kayhan* newspaper. Four of Iran's top generals and the prime minister had been executed by the revolutionary government. Their dead bodies were exhibited on the front page, lying on iron tables, with their naked chests exposed and their eyes wide open.

Looking at the photos made me feel cold and nauseated. I could see how all my bridges to the past, and to Iran, were falling down, and I'd been gone less than a month. I knew that what had started in Iran would not end easily or hastily.

I went to a jewelry shop on Fulham Road and asked the jeweler if he was interested in buying my jewels. After examining them, he gave me a rough price for my diamonds and rubies.

My mother called me soon after and told me that my aunt had finally arrived in London. Aunt Afsar had a nice apartment in Bayswater. She and I talked until dawn. She asked me to stay with her, but I told her I would rather live with English friends and converse in English. I also asked for her advice on the jewels, and she said the best place was on Sloane Street and within walking distance to the famous Harrods department store.

I took most of my jewels with me to the jewelry shop except for the ones that had sentimental value. I emptied the shoe bag containing the jewels, and the jeweler took a long time examining them. After what seemed like forever, he offered me 20,000 pounds and said that he would buy them right away. But he would not pay the same amount if I left the store and came back later.

I was being taken advantage of and I knew it. The jewels were worth much more, but I did not have time to go door to door to see who would pay the highest price. I needed the money now.

Besides, I was looking at the bigger picture. I wanted to go to university in England. I could live like a true student, economize, get my degree, and start working.

I took a moment and then pushed the jewels toward him, without even looking at them. I got the check, danced all the way to the bank, and went back to school.

There were a couple of newly migrated Iranians, like myself, at Berlitz. One of them was a cousin of an old friend named

Bijan. He was a talkative, energetic young man with a slight resemblance to the actor Adam Sandler. He said that a friend wanted to rent out his room at Brunel University in Uxbridge, West London, and sail around Europe in the summer. I loved the idea. I could live in a university for the summer and probably take summer classes in English.

I put all my belongings in my car and went to Brunel. It was a small room on the first floor with a single spring bed that had lost its elasticity. Two narrow rows of wooden shelves lined the wall, and a window overlooked a canopy of grass.

I started unpacking and was placing some of my belongings on the shelves when I noticed that people were running in the hall. I asked a couple of students what was going on, and they said, "Margaret Thatcher, our new prime minister, is about to give her inaugural speech. Come and watch it at the canteen with us."

I went with them and was in awe of her.

"There are rumors that I am an Iron Lady. Yes, I am an Iron Lady; tighten your belts, for we are going to change Britain for good," said the newly elected conservative prime minister. Not only did she change Britain for good, but she also changed me.

Up until then I had wanted to pursue acting, but all of a sudden I realized how I could be more useful to my family, friends, and the people of my country: by studying political science.

I STAYED AT my aunt's on the weekends and so did my cousins.

Hamid was nineteen and Roya was seventeen. They had both gone to boarding schools in England and were about to go to a university in Watford, in Hertfordshire, in the fall.

We were having dinner and discussing politics when I asked them about their school. They said that it was nice and had livable boarding facilities. I wondered what the university requirements were like, and Hamid suggested that I visit the International University of Europe, run mostly by American faculty.

The International University of Europe accepted my Iranian high school diploma (which I promised to get from home), but were also asking for a certificate in the English language.

Time was passing faster than light, and I needed to find a place in London and start getting ready for my first certificate in English. It would be issued by the University of Cambridge in a local examination held in late June.

I called my mother and asked her to send my diploma with my uncle, who was soon coming to London. Then I went back to Brunel University to pack up my belongings.

The school inspectors were going from room to room looking for illegal subletters. I threw all my belongings in a bed sheet and tossed it out the window. Next out the window was a pile of my books along with the small dictionaries from Iran in a suitcase. Last but not least was the spare tire to my car. I had used the car's trunk as storage and left the tire under the bed because it took up too much space in my car. The inspectors were almost at my door when I was finished throwing out my personal belongings.

The only way to save the tenant who had rented his room to me was to jump out the window, and so I did, just like in the movies, and landed on the grass. I did not land gracefully, but no harm was done. A couple of students helped me gather my things and disappear before anyone saw.

I went to the address that a friend had given me for an apartment in London. It was a two-story house that belonged to a middle-aged Iranian, Hajji, who had rented out most of his rooms to foreign students and was asking for fifty pounds a week. It was close to a great English school in North West London, in Golders Green. I gladly accepted it.

Hajji, the landlord, was nice but extremely stingy. He would get angry if we left the light on after ten o'clock or took too long in the shower; he kept reminding us how costly his water and power bills were. But I was happy to live in a house full of students from all over the world. I was studying at the Golders Green school for a first certificate in English.

I will never forget one of our teachers, a little old lady who taught reading, pronouncing the letter *W* as in "double *u*" and not like *V*. (Iranians traditionally pronounce the sound as "ve" instead of "we.")

She said, "Do not bite your lips when pronouncing the letter *W*. Round your lips and put a little bit of air in it."

22

BLENDING IN

As time went on, it became obvious that the Ayatollah had no intention of being a spiritual leader like Gandhi or of letting the people of Iran choose their own form of government like in the United States. He was a dictator, ambitious, and there to rule.

I phoned Aydin every time I could and managed to talk to him briefly, but often the communication lines were jammed or bugged. It was becoming increasingly frustrating.

It was time to sell my car, a green 250 CLK Mercedes-Benz. I loved my car and I had even a name for it, Sanjar, after a Persian hero's horse. I was worried for Sanjar and wanted to sell him to a good driver who would take proper care of him. I interviewed buyers over the phone. I asked one if he was a fast driver, and he got mad at me and said that it was none of my business. Finally I found a good buyer for Sanjar. He was in his seventies and lived in the country. He assured me that he would take care of the car and even offered me the opportunity to come visit Sanjar if I so chose.

I kept studying English and spending time with my aunt. My parents were so grateful that my aunt was close by. Aydin was also happy to see that I had decided to further educate myself. We both knew there was no place for me in the Islamic Republic, let alone the possibility of acting in Iran under such a political regime.

When I told my father that I had sold my jewelry and my car and was living off of the money, he asked me to go to the Iranian Embassy in London and apply for a student money exchange. That would allow my parents to send me the school tuition via the Iranian banks instead of through the black market.

I went to the embassy and followed my father's instructions. But I was told that I was supposed to have applied for it before leaving Iran. I called my father and told him the problem. He suggested I come home, for our New Year, and take care of it.

I discussed it with Aydin, and he was very happy. He said my father was right. I had missed Aydin and my family and friends and Pasha beyond belief. I knew I would need financial help sooner or later if I were to finish my planned four years of university. Besides, I needed to go back to Iran and see if I could perhaps live there again.

I WENT BACK to Iran in March 1980. As the government was actively interrogating actors, I traveled not under my husband's surname but rather used the one on my passport, my family name of Vaziritabar. That way the authorities would not know I was there. Aydin and Mahdi picked me up at the airport. I threw my arms around Aydin and hugged him like I might never let go of him again. When we got home, Pasha wiggled in delight, kissing me until I fell back on the floor. Aydin was happy to see me back at home, wrestling with Pasha. His mother was the happiest one of all.

My father and I went to the Ministry of Science at four in the morning the following day to file the application for a student allowance abroad. There was a line of students already waiting when we got there. We were permitted in at eight o'clock. The guard at the door looked at me and rudely asked me why I was wearing nail polish, which was forbidden. I politely responded that I was in Iran for a friend's wedding and that's why my nails were red. I said I never wore it otherwise. He let me in reluctantly. My father liked the way I handled the guard, but warned me, "What you see is the surface, the so-called calm before the chaos. But we see beneath it, things that you do not see and cannot even imagine. Young people like you are being tortured for conspiracy against the regime. Kids, who are helping the various underground oppositions, distributing newsletters against the regime, are now thrown into Evin Prison and God knows what they do to them. Go back, get your B.A. and we'll see. But do not stay here."

My father was right. The scene in Tehran resembled a ghost town at high noon in a western, awaiting a long-drawn-out gun battle. People were functioning, but it seemed as if they were holding their breath. They must have known what was going on in the torture chambers of the regime, like my father did.

Yet they did not talk about it. *Hijab* was not mandatory yet, but it was lurking in the shadows. Muslim fundamentalists' were celebrating their victory.

I had seen a couple of friends but had not seen Abbas Nal-bandian, the head of the workshop, and I had not heard any-thing from Dokhi, the friend with whom we'd visited Italy along with her husband, Behnam, the other half of the four musketeers. She had not contacted me since I left. I had called her a couple of times but did not get through. She had visited her brother in the U.S.A. and would send me postcards wher-ever she went. Her last one came from New York, saying she was going to explore South America with a couple of friends, but that was months ago. I told Aydin that I was going to Dokhi's house to find out where she was. He asked me to sit down.

Dokhi had had a brain stroke in Brazil right after the revolu-tion and died. She was only twenty-eight years old. Her mother did her best to bring her body back to Iran, but by the time the international police had located her, Dokhi was already buried in a Muslim cemetery on the outskirts of a village in northern Brazil.

The Muslim cemetery did not allow the removal of the body due to Islamic law. When at last the permission was given in light of extraordinary circumstances, a huge flood had washed out the whole cemetery, taking all the stones, the dirt, and the corpses into a valley of wild tulips.

This was what Dokhi had always wanted, to become one with nature. She was not afraid of death. She thought it was a passage that takes humans back to nature.

I could not believe it. I cried all day and night. I could hardly breathe when I went to bed. Aydin sat on the bed with a book in his hand and recited Omar Khayyam's poetry for Pasha and me until the sun rose. I still do not want to believe Dokhi is dead and have followed women who looked like her on three occasions in London, Amsterdam, and Paris.

I wanted to visit Abbas Nalbandian, but I had to see what had happened to the workshop first. It was indeed a terrible sight: the revolutionary government had shut down the workshop, and its entrance was covered with bricks and mud.

But the sight of Abbas's dark and stuffy small apartment was even worse. He had been interrogated in jail about a handgun and a book—Mao Tse-tung's essays on communism and Marxism—which the police had found in his locker at the workshop. Others at the workshop knew that both items belonged to someone else, but Nalbandian had refused to name names and had probably paid the price. He was now dangerously thin and vulnerable.

I did not dare ask him about the interrogations. Instead I asked if he wanted me to make a nice omelet with tomato, his favorite, and eat together, like the old days. He agreed and had a few bites before he passed out from the various painkillers and tranquilizers he had been given. He slept on his stomach, his head tilted to the left, breathing softly. I sat in his small living room, where he had spread his mattress. He refused to sleep in the bedroom since being in jail at the notorious Evin political prison, where the regime interrogated and tortured innocent civilians for having different beliefs or ideologies. I looked at him in despair, feeling awful for not being able to do more for him. I left when Mahdi arrived. He, too, was extremely sad.

Abbas Nalbandian eventually committed suicide. He was said to have mixed an excessive dose of his sleeping pills with alcohol. And with him went another part of my past.

I had decided to stay only two weeks, but what came next made me leave even sooner.

I was visiting an actor friend of mine. She asked me how on earth I had not yet been summoned to the authorities. She said the revolutionary government was looking into every artist's dossier. She said a well-known female singer, a popular actress, and a director's wife had already been interrogated and were both under house arrest.

I was so thankful I was there under my father's name, but to be safe, I decided to return to London quickly.

I left again with a thousand sorrows. Somehow I knew this was it. The airport was chaotic. Passengers had to be dropped by the main entrance. Their families and friends did not get to see them to the terminal.

I got out, hugged my brother Shahriar and Aydin, and then turned around and did not look back until inside the terminal. My face was wet with tears. I cried the whole way to London, despite all the kindness of the Iran Air stewardesses. It was a far shorter journey than the one I had last taken out of Iran.

My father called a week later to tell me not to call home. He said the Comiteh, the self-appointed militia, had been to my parents' home looking for me as word of mouth had spread that I had been there. Iranians were spying on one another.

THANK GOD FOR my new friends. A couple of them were going to Valencia, a beautiful city in Spain. They had rented an apartment and invited me to join them for the summer. We had a lovely time swimming, cooking, and partying in our little apartment. I did the shopping and loved going to the market to smell the scents of the vegetables and fruits.

One day I was at the butcher shop, one of my favorite places in the market. The butcher was a broad-shouldered woman in her late thirties, chubby with strong hands.

"Good morning," I said. She smiled and said something in Spanish while rubbing her bloody butcher knife on her white apron.

"*Shah muerto*," she said. I looked at her in disbelief. She said it again. "*Shah muerto*." This time she drew an imaginary line on her throat signifying death. But I understood what she said. I was paralyzed, hoping I had misheard her. I had not.

The Shah had passed away from non-Hodgkin's lymphoma in 1980 at the age of sixty. Iran had lost a man who sincerely loved her. And I, for one, was bewildered, as were many others. If there was once a ray of hope to bring the monarchy back to Iran, it was now nothing but a shattered dream.

I PASSED THE exam for my first certificate in English in June 1981. I was now ready to go to college.

In autumn, I matriculated into the International University of Europe, in the city of Watford, to study international relations. I was extremely happy. My professors were mostly young, enthusiastic, and quite caring, and the faculty was incredibly supportive. I cut my hair short and started running in the morning.

Studying hard got me through the first year, but in the second year I was afraid of not being able to finish. The Iranian Embassy had refused to extend my governmental-tuition plan, claiming they would only allow three categories of students abroad to receive the governmental exchange rate: medical, engineering, and farming students.

BY THIS TIME I had discovered the Speakers' Corner in Hyde Park, on the corner of Park Lane and Cumberland Gate, where speakers and listeners have been gathering since the Royal Parks and Gardens Act of 1872 to share their political views, shed light on the injustices in the world through political awareness, and make changes. It is well known for hosting political leaders such as Karl Marx and Lenin. Any individual can stand up on a box and share his views with the world. I joined the thousands of demonstrators at Hyde Park Corner in one of the biggest demonstrations against the Islamic Republic in Iran. It was organized by the followers of Shapour Bakhtiar, the last prime minister of Iran. We walked all the way to Tottenham Court Road, about an hour and a half away on our slow-moving feet. We chanted in unison, "We want freedom for Iran, freedom and democracy. Political prisoners must be freed!" And we carried banners that said: "The youth of Iran are now being captured and tortured," "The world must pay attention to the injustices in Iran," "Down with religious tyranny!"

MY FINANCIAL SITUATION was deteriorating. I did not want to ask Aydin for any help. He had done his best, and it was time to let him get on with his own life, even though I still missed him madly. Besides, I did not want him to pay for my decisions. I was still legally his wife and was participating in these huge demonstrations against the regime.

I loved Aydin so much that I decided to leave him and not put him in harm's way. I did not even call him, in case his phone was bugged. I wrote him a lengthy letter, saying I wished I could live with him again but that I could not conform to religious tyranny. I knew I would put both of us in deep danger if I went back home. In addition, I had now tasted life in a democratic world, and I liked how it felt—more than returning to my husband. I was mature now. I had become logical. First and foremost I needed an education and then maybe I would one day be able to help the people of Iran. The path to enlightenment was far more enticing than traveling this path with another.

"Look for a path rather than path finder," Grandma used to say.

A few weeks later, Aydin and my father went to a law office in Tehran with my letter requesting a divorce.

I NOW WAS sharing a furnished apartment with a school friend. It had two stories and a tall church ceiling with a huge piano next to the large window on the second floor. There were two small French windows on the first floor facing a backyard, adjacent to a communal garden and playground. The owner of the apartment was a composer and was living in Austria for a couple of years. The address was 40 Warwick Avenue, near the BBC network.

I was at my new home when my mother called and gave me the news. She said, "You are divorced now." I said, "Thank you," and hung up. I felt like an astronaut whose tether had slipped from his space capsule. I felt numb, but my gut was twirling. I decided to take a walk and went to Hampstead Heath, where I cried for what was now a lost love. More pieces of my past were crumbling away.

23

MAHDI AND THE SHAH

SINCE I DID not want my parents to purchase pounds on the black market, I looked for a part-time job. A friend of mine was working at Browns boutique in Knightsbridge, well known for such couture lines as Donna Karan, Sonia Rykiel, and many more.

Its owner, Mr. Bernstein, was a Holocaust survivor. He was proud of the faded-blue serial numbers on his wrist, bitter evidence of his days as a captive in the Nazi camps, from the age of seventeen to nineteen.

Mr. Bernstein hired me to work part-time at the shop, where I saw many princesses and movie stars, as well as high-society socialites. I worked a full day on Saturdays and any other free nonschool days, including holidays and in the summer, when many of the other employees took their vacations.

At the back of the shop, next to the stockroom, was a kitchenette where girls or sales assistants would often rest during their lunch hour or fifteen-minute tea break twice a day. I either studied during lunch or took a quick walk on our street, which was in the fashion district, to see what other designers had on display. Knowing the market and understanding high fashion helped me to better assist my wealthy customers and therefore make more money, as our salaries were based on a percentage of our sales.

If a client couldn't find something at Browns, I told her where to go in order to find it. Mr. Bernstein once asked me if I had sent a client to Valentino. I told him the truth, how I was trying to maintain trustworthy relations with our clientele, and he loved the idea.

I started getting worried about my finances again the following summer. Aydin had given me the two pieces of calligraphy we purchased in Egypt and asked me to keep them for a rainy day.

I called a dear friend of ours, Dr. Jazayeri, a scholar in Persian art and antiquities, and asked for his advice. He introduced me to Mr. Saeedi, the head of the Asian Art Department at Sotheby's on Bond Street.

Mr. Saeedi loved both calligraphies, especially the one by Mir Emad. Both pieces were picked up for Sotheby's upcoming calligraphy auction. The Mir Emad started off with a £1,500 bid, and the starting price for the other was £700. Dr. Jazayeri and I attended the auction. There were about twenty people in the room. The Mir Emad was up for auction first. As I heard the auctioneer announcing the work, I was taken back to the day Aydin and I had found the piece in Cairo's old bazaar. I started to think about Aydin and how he had gotten married again to a beautiful lady a year after our divorce. They now had a son, Takin. His new wife did not like me and denied having any connection to me when asked if I were related to the family. But if they asked Aydin, he once told me, he would say, "Yes, I had the pleasure of being her husband."

"Fifteen hundred pounds," said the auctioneer, awaiting bids. "Seventeen hundred," said an Arab gentleman in his fifties, neatly dressed in traditional white clothes.

"Two thousand," said a Chinese man.

A second later, the battle of bids became more heated: three thousand, four thousand, five thousand! Dr. Jazayeri was stunned. He looked at me and said that obviously two collectors were in tight competition. Then we heard the auctioneer call out six thousand.

That alone would have covered my tuition for two semesters at college, meaning I would be able to go to the fourth and final year and get my B.A.

The Mir Emad sold for 7,500 pounds, and the other went for 3,500 pounds.

My third year in college was the best one of all. I had made new friends and my brother Shahram joined me in London to continue with his architecture degree. He had been accepted at Oxford University for his doctorate. He moved in with me, and the two of us studied together. It was nice being around family again.

I WAS WORKING at Browns on a rainy Saturday afternoon when a woman came in, soaking wet. She was looking for a cocktail dress. Our manager, Christine, asked me to help the lady, so I took her downstairs to show her our dresses. She looked at me and said, "Are you Shohreh?"

"Yes, I am," I said. She said she was Mahdi's cousin. I was so happy to see her. I had not heard from Mahdi for a couple of months. I wondered how he was doing. The woman apologized for being the bearer of bad news: Mahdi had taken his life the same way Abbas from the workshop had, with a combination of sleeping pills and alcohol. He'd gotten into a verbal fight with his superior, an illiterate informant in a key position at Iranian National Television. He had cursed the Ayatollah and all his informants. He was then taken to jail for a couple of months. Finally he was released with severe depression. His sister found him and took him to a hospital, but it was too late—he died there a few hours after he was brought in. Mahdi was thirty-four years old.

I did not know how to react or what to say, except for wanting to crash to the floor. The woman left, and I started crying like hell. Christine gave me the rest of the day off. I went home sobbing and called Aydin later that night. It was true. Aydin had gone to Mahdi's deathbed.

IRAN HAD BEEN in a bloody war with its neighboring country Iraq, beginning in September 1980 when Ba'athist Iraq attacked Iran after years of border disputes and fear of a Shiite insurgency motivated by the Iranian revolution. The eight-year war planted the fundamental pillars of the religious tyranny that exists in Iran today. War brings countries together and its people closer, therefore no one was left to question the government.

I once asked Aydin how his family dealt with the war, and he said they played games like Monopoly in the basement while Iraqi bombs poured from the sky.

My friends were dying one by one. I had never felt so lonely and helpless in my life. I worried for my mother and father, as well as millions of Iranians who now lived their lives in extreme caution, behind closed, thick dark curtains.

24

ELIXIR OF LOVE?

M Y FOURTH YEAR in school was the fastest one of all. I was swamped by books, newspapers, pens and pencils, highlighters, and working at Browns, and then suddenly it was graduation day. I felt like I had achieved something that once looked like a mirage. I invited a couple of friends and my cousins to my big day. I was graduating at the age of thirty-two but felt like a twenty-one-year-old in my black gown and tasseled hat.

Finally my name was called out. I got up to get my diploma and changed the direction of the tassel on my hat, from the left to the right. The direction of my life had changed as well.

Or so I thought.

I WAS NOW working full-time at Browns while I looked for a job in a media outlet. I was preparing for an interview at my favorite newspaper, *The Guardian*, when Parviz Kardan, a prominent Iranian actor and director who had also immigrated to London, called me and asked if I would like to play a lead in his play. That little actress in me woke up instantly and said, "Why not bring the script over and let me read it?"

I read the play and fell in love with it. It was a political play (ah, my major would get some good use) revolving around a calligrapher's life in exile.

There were only two characters. Kardan was to portray the calligrapher while also directing the play, and I would portray the woman, whom the calligrapher meets at an Iranian gathering in London. But the calligrapher tells her that he has lost all his belongings. He explains that he has been condemned to death in postrevolutionary Iran for being the Shah's personal calligrapher but managed to flee the country.

Living in exile, and witnessing all the injustices in Iran, makes him want to send a message to the international media for refusing to shed light on the truth. His plan is to jump off the woman's balcony with an open letter to the media in his pocket, where it would be easily found after his death. Perhaps this act would draw attention from the British media. In the end the woman convinces him that going to the media directly would be the more powerful way to help his people.

I must confess that the play gave me a totally new perspective on politics and arts, and how interwoven they can be in real life. I had seen it in the movies but had never experienced it firsthand. The thought of the enormous possibilities, of portraying politics through the arts, was overwhelming and surely more challenging to me than becoming a politician, as I had planned. I could be far more beneficial to my people doing what I knew best—acting.

I decided to do the play. I was still at Browns and rehearsed in the evenings for a month and a half. I owed a sum of three thousand pounds to the university and had to pay it back in order to receive my B.A. certificate (which had been taken back after I left the podium), so that I could apply for jobs. Working at Browns would have taken me months to pay the university back. But maybe the play could help me make the money sooner?

Rainbow, which was in Farsi, opened in June 1984, at the Polish Cultural Center in London, a great venue for the average theatergoer, conveniently located next to a train station. It seated close to four hundred people and had an intimate feeling to it.

Our premiere was very emotional. Iranians had come to see the play from everywhere in the United Kingdom. Many of our friends also came from afar to support us. I was mesmerized by the sight of our audience. They were cheering and clapping. We received a standing ovation every night.

The play paid off, and I paid the tuition due at the university. I got my B.A. and took a few weeks off from my work at Browns. Kardan and I started a tour around Europe through Paris, Nice, Munich, Frankfurt, and Brussels. We were both relaxed about the trip and were never stressed over delays as we traveled through Europe, living out of our suitcases. Fortunately we did not have many props except for a large oil painting of Big Ben, which we used as a backdrop. The rest were replicas of antique French furniture in the woman's apartment, which we rented locally.

Iranians abroad were more than thrilled to see the play. They told us they had not seen a Farsi-language play (or an Iranian play) in years, let alone in exile, and encouraged us to do it more often.

Kardan received a call regarding a tour in the U.S.A., starting in Los Angeles, home of the largest Iranian population outside of Iran. I was thrilled to visit Los Angeles and to catch up with a couple of friends who had fled there.

I WAS NOW in the homeland of all the American actors I had idolized from the films and television shows of my youth. Seeing the enormous HOLLYWOOD sign sent jitters through my body. I was in a country that defined freedom and valued democracy.

Our first performance at the Horace Mann Theater was sold out days before. And the number of people who showed up was way beyond the capacity of the theater. I was getting ready in a dressing room when they told me that the audience had charged in and broken a huge window at the entrance. My immediate thought was, this is the place I want to live, where the audience breaks down the doors to see a play! Although a cliché, I thought to myself, God bless America.

Kardan and I traveled throughout the U.S.A., performing in New York, D.C., Chicago, Miami, and San Francisco.

EVENTUALLY WE RETURNED to Los Angeles, and I rented a studio on Ohio Street in Westwood, next to U.C.L.A. One of my colleagues at the workshop in Tehran, Houshang Touzie, was in Los Angeles promoting his first film abroad, *The Messenger.* Houshang was quite good-looking, like Rob Lowe meets Tommy Lee Jones, with a nice build and brooding eyes.

He came to see the play, and occasionally we went on cultural outings together. When he was younger, I used to think he was too much of a ladies' man. Now he seemed much more mature and looked me squarely in the eyes—instead of at all the beautiful ladies swooning about him. Houshang was familiar with the town, and he had a car.

I asked him why he was still a bachelor, and he told me that he had divorced his wife in New York and had come to stay in Los Angeles to start his own theater company.

An Iranian celebrity friend of mine had asked me if I would introduce her to Houshang, and I did. We went to a party at the woman's home and I took them out on the balcony and left them alone. Five minutes later Houshang came back to me and told me to stop it. He said he was perfectly capable of finding a girl for himself. We laughed.

A few Farsi-speaking TV shows aired weekly on an international channel in Los Angeles. One of them offered me a job as a talk show host commenting on the social and political environment in Iran. I was not quite sure if I wanted to move so fast, and my British student visa was about to expire. I asked for a rain check and left Los Angeles by the end of the summer of 1984.

LONDON WAS COLD and looked strange to me. I missed the sunshine in California. I went back to Browns and worked harder than ever, trying to figure out what to do next. I was thirty-three years old and wanted to get married and have children. Arts and politics were now my life and my passion, but the urge to have a baby and a family was so strong that I decided to share the news with my friends.

I told them that I was ready to get married and asked them

to look for a good suitor for me. At first my friends thought I was joking, but they agreed to do it once they saw how serious I was.

My first suitor, "Mr. K," was a tall, fairly good-looking, thirty-five-year-old businessman. He was a self-made man and had managed to accumulate a good fortune for himself. He had recently purchased a luxurious three-bedroom apartment, with tall ceilings and long halls, in a Victorian building on Kensington High Street. He worked from home, and all day long he bought and sold stuff over the phone.

He told me he had been looking for an interior designer for his apartment and had decided to ask me to decorate it. I thought it was a nice gesture: he wanted me to decorate our future home.

My father was right: I am a soldier of my work. I went to work every day at Browns and took my lunch hours to find Mr. K the best available furniture and decorative items.

Harrods and Harvey Nichols were both around the corner from Sloane Street, where Browns was located. I found most of the furniture in those stores. I also discovered a few antiques, including a large, early-1900s painting of a saint on glass on Portobello Road, my favorite antique market in London. It was a great buy, and with the purchase of a couple of cushions, the mission was done. The end result was that the apartment looked chic and posh, without having taken too much effort.

Mr. K invited me to Milan and then to Greece, to the beautiful island of Mykonos. I gladly accepted.

He told me one night that he had a business idea for the both of us. Milan produces the best lingerie in the world, and he wanted to import Italian lingerie to London. Would I be willing to start a business together? With his experience and my salesmanship, we would be a great team—I thought.

This time I spent all my lunch hours, evenings, and weekends at a variety of stores. From luxurious, expensive places like Harrods to mass producers like Marks & Spencer, I examined every piece of lingerie and took careful notes. Mr. K had made me a chart to record the color, size, quality, and price of every item. He believed that one should always study the market first. His plan was to import a line of lingerie that would have the look of an expensive one but cost a lot less, something he said the present market was lacking. Our survey had proved to us that there was a huge price gap between cheap cotton pants and silk ones, and there was nothing in the middle that could serve the emerging middle class.

My parents came to visit my brother and me for a few weeks. I had already made plans with Mr. K for the holidays but would be gone only ten days. Mr. K asked me to invite my family to his home before we left. I got there early to see if he needed any help. He was thankful and asked me to help with grocery shopping. I opened the refrigerator, and it was completely empty except for a bottle of mineral water. The two of us headed to the nearest grocery store.

While I was picking out fruits, he kept asking me the price of every item. It was weird; a man who was willing to pay a couple of thousand pounds for furniture was looking for bargains at the grocery store. But maybe that was how he had managed to make such a lavish life for himself at such a young age. He economized whenever and wherever he could.

My parents loved him. My mother thought he was polite

and charming, and my father was quite taken by his education and relentless efforts to become such a successful businessman in Britain.

Mr. K and I left the day after. Milan was magnificent, and so was the magical world of the fashion industry. We went to a lingerie fashion show for three days, starting at eleven o'clock in the morning and ending at four o'clock in the afternoon. It was located in a thirty-thousand-square-foot, three-story industrial building. Tall and gorgeous Italian models were scattered among the crowd on each floor, walking around in their underwear and revealing bras. For shopping purposes, buyers could touch the materials but not the models, nor could they talk to them. Mr. K and I touched as many underwear as we could for two days and ordered dozens of samples.

We went sightseeing in the early evening and dined at a variety of restaurants. Mr. K liked shopping around for food. He read the restaurants' menus (and, I assumed, their prices) displayed on their windows thoroughly.

We flew to Athens next and stayed with a relative of his in a beautiful villa in the suburbs. We flew to Mykonos a day later.

Mr. K was a regular visitor to the island. He rented a certain bungalow from a short, heavy, and talkative Greek woman named Helen who took care of a colony of bungalows by the beach. Mr. K had asked her to provide us with some fruit and a bottle of wine, which we shared with her.

Later on we dined at a restaurant with a great view of the island and strolled through the alleys, watching tourists dancing to the familiar melody from *Zorba the Greek*, or singing their own favorite songs in outdoor cafés.

The moon was full and the cobalt blue sea was calm. Drunken young lovers were everywhere.

Suddenly, I was having a change of heart over Mr. K and some of his peculiar ways. He knew I wanted to follow my dream of acting, but he did not care enough to talk about it. And now he wanted to start a business with me, a rather active business that required a lot of time and supervision. Who was this person? What if I needed to go on the road again? I kept asking myself all sorts of questions as I went to sleep that night.

The next morning, I woke up late. Mr. K was already up and about and talking to Helen. They stopped when I got closer. Helen hugged me and congratulated me. Mr. K had told her we were getting married, and she suggested we do it on the island. She had gone to the only church in town to register us. I was speechless and told him that my parents would be upset. Since it was my second marriage, they did not expect a huge wedding, only a formal wedding party. Mr. K said we would throw the party in London, and we went to buy the rings. But all of this was moving a little fast for me.

Those who have been to Mykonos know that the island is famous for its restaurants, bars, and jewelry shops. Brand names like Cartier and Boucheron and Rolex, Greek designers like Zolotas and Lalaounis, and tons of small jewelry shops located close together. We walked for a while, skipping the brand names, and stepped into a shop literally eight-by-ten feet in size.

Mr. K had decided that Russian rings were the best and asked the shopkeeper to show us some. Mr. K took a long look and picked the tiniest of them all. He asked the seller to engrave our names and the date in our rings.

My father, Anushiravan Vaziritabar. "Do not punish children, love them and treat them with dignity, so they would know better," said my father.

My mother Eftekhar Al-Sadat, a woman of substance and courage.

My mother was obsessed with framing our photos and displaying them all around the house. This photo was taken at my mother's favorite photographer's studio, the Photo Gallery Sayeh.

My brothers and me, planted in front of the camera, again at the Photo Gallery Sayeh.

My first attempt at modeling at my mother's hair salon. This photo was taken by the show's photographer, Balasanian.

My wedding with Aydin at my aunt's orchard in northern Tehran. The gentleman in the background is Aydin's best friend and our first landlord, Bijan Khorsand. (*Photo by Photo Gallery Sayeh*)

The cast of the workshop's production of *The Pot Lady and Mash Rahim*, including my future husband, Houshang Touzie, to my left. Who knew we were going to fall in love in the years to come?

Me as the bondmaid in *The Chess Game of the Wind*, directed by Mohammad Reza Aslani.

A shot from *Broken Hearts*, directed by Ali Hatami, the film to which I owe my fame in Iran. It was the only film I was a part of there that was released publicly and not censored.

Pasha, content, resting,
taking a moment
to himself after
having tangoed to
Albinoni's entire *Adagio*
with me.

Aydin and me in Venice,
Italy, enjoying our last
days together in February
1979. The Polaroid
photo was taken by our
travel companion and
dear fiend Mahdi Kafaie.

Graduation day, 1984,
and I am ready to put
my degree to use.

The Pot Lady, my flower shop on
the corner of Santa Monica
and Westwood, named after one of my
favorite roles in *The Pot Lady
and Mash Rahim*, written and directed
by Ishmael Khalag.

I am married to my
prince charming,
Houshang, in L.A.
(*Photo by Mike Chitsaz
photography*)

Houshang, Tara, and I
knew our family dynamics
from the start. This photo
was taken by our friend
and neighbor Farhad
Zanichkhah.

Tara and me, exploring the magnificent Yellowstone National Park. This photo was taken by my late friend Mahwash.

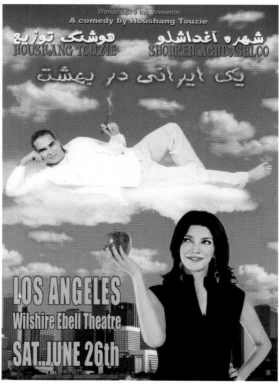

Workshop79 Inc presents
A comedy by Houshang Touzie

شهره آغداشلو
SHOHREH AGHDASHLOO

هوشنگ توزیع
HOUSHANG TOUZIE

یک ایرانی در بهشت

LOS ANGELES
Wilshire Ebell Theatre
SAT..JUNE 26th

Our latest play, *An Iranian in Paradise*, written and directed by Houshang Touzie in 2012. (*Photo by Syrus Kerdooni*)

The iconic portrait of me
by Aydin Aghdashloo.
The Latin inscription reads:
"To Shohreh,
my beloved wife, Aydin."
(*Photo by Abbas Hojat-Panah*)

A love alley in northern Tehran, January 2013.
(*Photo by Hanieh Vaziritabar*)

The witty Greek jeweler smirked and said: "Would you like me to add your love story to it?" Mr. K replied, "It's not necessary."

Mr. K then asked the price, and the jeweler said that the rings and the engraving cost $400.

"How about three hundred and fifty?" asked Mr. K.

"I do not bargain with my craft, sir. Take it or leave it," said the jeweler.

Mr. K was embarrassed and agreed to pay the full price.

When we went back to our bungalow to change for dinner, Helen was waiting for us. She said that in order to be able to marry on the island we needed to convert to the Greek Orthodox religion first.

"What is the procedure like?" I asked.

"It is very easy," explained Helen. "You follow the priest's prayers and say a few words, and then they will stamp your passports. It will not take more than an hour, and then you can get married at the church." Mr. K was happy to do it and asked Helen to wake us up at ten the following morning.

We went to dinner, and I was on the verge of a nervous breakdown. I am a people person and love socializing. But there is one kind of person I cannot stand: stingy ones. I despise those who bargain with poor vendors. Life is much too short for that.

There was no way I was going to marry Mr. K. Culturally I was too shy to break my promise. Fortunately, I have always been able to think quickly on my feet.

"Are you not worried about your trips to Iran?" I asked at dinner.

"What about Iran?" he said.

I said that the Greek Orthodox stamps in his passport may prevent him from visiting Iran.

"You would be considered a minority in Iran if nothing else," I said. "Why take such a risk when we can easily get married at home in London?"

I told him that, personally, I would not mind converting, for I am interested in all religions, like my grandmother. I am fascinated by Jesus, too, but I was not the one who was going to travel to Iran. "I will never go back to Iran until it is free," I told Mr. K.

While cleaning his now steamy glasses, he said that he had not thought about that. I knew I had hit the right button, so I kept on talking about all the ramifications of marrying on the island.

We spent the next day sunbathing and reading—rather than getting married. I planned on breaking up with him upon our return to London.

25

THE PRINCESS
AND THE SHOP

I CAME BACK from Mykonos and ran to Browns, knowing that I needed to keep working until I could find the right path—and the right man—for me.

It was during this time at Browns that I had the pleasure of seeing Princess Diana in person. Our boss, Mr. Bernstein, called the shop in advance and instructed us to wait for her arrival. He asked us not to bother her with the frequently asked question "Can I help you."

"She will ask for help, if she needs any," said Mr. Bernstein.

Being familiar with the Iranian monarchy, I was expecting a herd of secret service to pour in first. But she came with only two bodyguards, who stayed at the door. The shop was not closed to the public for her visit, upon her own request.

She came in, and although I was trying not to look at her and to let her feel free, I could not help myself. She was not only beautiful and fragile, with her lovely British porcelain skin, but she also had an amazing presence and the most charming shy smile I have ever seen in my life. I had watched her getting married to her Prince Charming on television not long before and had wished her a long and happy marriage.

She went through the racks and looked at a variety of evening gowns and dresses. She then turned around and thanked us. Her visit did not take more than twenty minutes, but she knew exactly what she wanted, and that item was going to be delivered to the palace later.

I HAD MANAGED to save some money from the tour in the U.S.A. and was thinking it might be a good idea to go back to university and get my master's degree in political science.

I had applied to a couple of universities and was waiting to hear back when Massud Assadolahi, another Iranian actor-director, called and told me about his play titled *The Mirror*. This was the story of a writer and his wife who are robbed by human smugglers. Marooned in Pakistan without any money, they manage to obtain refugee visas to England. Having lost everything, including their identities, brings them to the point of no return. Once again I was being tested. Perhaps my destiny was being offered on a silver platter.

Out of sheer coincidence, I had read an article concerning Iranians fleeing Iran, and how they were often the victims of human smugglers. Some were even murdered for their money.

I agreed to do the play, knowing it would take me back to America. It managed to attract a Farsi-speaking audience again and the recent Iranian immigrants who looked forward to watching a play starring their favorite actors in exile. This time I decided to research the possibility of living in Los Angeles.

I had met a young woman at a friend's party on my first trip to Los Angeles and had quite liked her. Her nickname was Mimi. She was in her late twenties, tall and beautiful. She had told me I could always move in with her if I ever decided to return to L.A. Mimi was working at a shoe boutique on Sunset and was also being helped financially by her brother in Europe. She was about to leave her partner of a year and needed to move out. We found a beautiful two-bedroom apartment off of Westwood Boulevard. I had to sign the lease alone, because her credit score was poor.

I was alarmed that her credit was so bad but decided to go ahead and move in with her anyway. I visited a couple of boutiques on the Sunset Strip in search of employment, and they were all more than happy to hire me, especially when I told them that I had a letter of recommendation from Browns. It gave me confidence to know that if acting didn't work out, I could have a job at a nice store.

I kept exploring my options while Mimi was at work and partied with her in the evening. She loved drinking at night and found an excuse to celebrate any occasion. I drank, too, but was not very fond of alcohol. Mimi would come home and tell me that her brother had expanded his business in France and that it called for a celebration. She would dash out and return with a small bottle of booze—brandy, vodka, or tequila, depending on her financial situation. I did not mind drinking wine occasionally, but after a week or two I realized that Mimi was an alcoholic.

IT WAS 1986, and I knew becoming an actor in Hollywood was more than wishful thinking. With my accent and my jet-black hair, I was not exactly the girl next door. So, what else could I do to guarantee a regular income? I had to make sure that I would not end up living on the street when my savings ran out.

My grandmother told bedtime stories, mostly based on Persian fairy tales and fables. Regrettably I could not understand the meaningful messages hidden in those bedtime stories at the time, or at least not until I started living on my own and gaining life experience. One of my favorites, still, is the story of "The Prince and the Rug."

ONCE UPON A time, there was a handsome, courageous prince, the only heir to the throne. He lived in a castle in a magical land, overlooking a valley of clouds. The castle was made of a fine multitude of colored marbles gathered from all over the world, covered by turquoise domes laid on golden pillars.

His father, the king, wanted him to become a warrior, and his mother, the queen, insisted that the prince should also learn the art of rug weaving in his spare time. Everyone at the court was astonished at the queen's demand, for weaving rugs was far beneath the royal prince.

"Only village girls weave rugs," the poor prince cried. But after all he had to obey the queen and learned the craft.

The prince even designed a rug for his mother. It was a royal-size saffron-colored rug with a huge paisley in the center, surrounded by green leaves, and the prince's signature woven into it.

Years later, on his eighteenth birthday, the prince got lost while exploring the forest with his attendants. He kept wandering around, desperately looking for the path that had brought him there. Exhausted, the prince bathed in a steamy spring, praying in the moonlight. He slept inside the trunk of an ancient tree next to his horse tied to one of the thousands of branches of the tree.

The next morning he kept riding in the vast, emerald green forest, passing trees, steamy springs, and wildflower bushes that all looked alike, as though he were riding in a maze, until he found himself in a foreign land, where the natives spoke a different language and worshiped different gods.

The prince sold his horse first, to survive, then his jewels, and finally his royal clothing. Left with a faded caftan, he became a wanderer on the streets. Tired and hungry he found himself in front of a rug shop.

He entered quietly and started looking around. An old man was restoring a rug next to a pile of rugs in the corner. The prince used his little knowledge of this new language and asked the old man for a job. The old man gladly accepted but told him that he could only offer food and shelter in return.

The prince started working right away, and in just a few months he managed to make a name for himself and started designing rugs. His work was excellent, and the royal court of the foreign land ordered a special rug for a special friend of the court.

The nostalgic prince designed a rug similar to the one he had made for his mother, the queen, and wove his signature in it. The royal court sent the saffron-colored carpet with a huge paisley in the center of it to the king of the magical land, as a token of appreciation for the peace and prosperity in the region.

When the queen of the magical land saw the rug, she realized that her son was alive. She stopped mourning and started looking for him. She ordered the royal court to send a team of warriors to find the prince in the faraway land, and they did. The king and the queen came to take him home, and when they realized how he had survived, the queen laughed and said, "Now you know why I always wanted you to learn the craft."

OH, HOW I wished I had listened to Grandma's bedtime stories thoroughly rather than getting captured in their atmospheric realm, so I, too, would have learned a craft that would help me survive in a faraway land.

I decided to start a small business in L.A. Many of my friends had started small businesses and were very successful. I had managed to save $20,000 while working in London and was able to secure a similar amount in a loan from Barclays Bank.

After a few weeks of thorough research, especially in the Santa Monica and Westwood areas where Iranian immigrants had found a safe haven after the revolution, I noticed that there were not many flower shops. I decided that would be it, I would open a flower shop. When I shared the idea with my friends all I heard was positive feedback. "Do it as soon as you can," they said.

In my younger life in Iran I was surrounded by people who had an extraordinary love for flowers. My mother and grandfather were both fascinated by flowers. Grandpa knew exactly how many rosebuds were on the bushes in his garden, counting them every single morning, all year round. He would lose his mind if anybody touched the buds or somehow broke a branch.

He would call all of the children to the backyard and interrogate us while our parents joyfully watched. We would all deny any wrongdoing, and he would walk away muttering, "One of these days I am going to catch the traitor and only God knows what I am going to do to him."

After a couple of weeks I managed to find a small storefront on the corner of Westwood and Santa Monica, very close to my apartment on Ohio Street. It had been a warehouse and was located at the back of an Iranian restaurant called Deezzy, named after a special Persian meal with meat.

The building had character and was said to have a lot of potential. I rented the place for five years under one condition: I would either leave or sublet it after one year if the business did not work. The gentleman who rented the place to me owned Deezzy. He knew me from my films and plays in Iran and did his best to accommodate me.

I named the shop Pot Lady, after the play I had performed all those years ago. I thought that with a little investment I would be able to create my own business and generate some income. I was lucky enough to find a partner, Misha, a single, shy red-headed Iranian mother with a pleasant smile and two adorable young kids. Misha and I started exploring the flower market in downtown Los Angeles and kept looking for a florist, an artist who had studied the magic of designing flowers. We finally found her.

Her name was Kian, a blond Iranian woman with an incredible resemblance to one of my favorite actors, Faye Dunaway. She was a Laura Ashley type, wearing loose floral skirts and pastel tops. Kian had taken a course in flower design in Paris in the 1970s to decorate her own house and the lavish parties she threw back in Iran. Now she had to design flower arrangements to survive.

She had been married to a senator and had a great life in Iran, but like millions of Iranians, she had immigrated to America. She lived in a modest apartment in the Westwood area close to the flower shop. She did not drive but could easily walk to work.

Misha and I went to the flower market at five o'clock every other morning to purchase fresh flowers and those on Kian's list for special orders. We opened the shop around nine. Misha and Kian would stay at the shop while I visited local restaurants, cafés, shops, and other businesses that might be willing to buy our flowers.

The problem was that small businesses could not afford fresh flowers, and the big businesses already had accounts with well-known flower suppliers, mostly with our large competitor, Mayflowers. Another problem we encountered was the delivery of the ordered flowers. The cost of using a professional delivery service was too high and I did not drive—or, I confess, I was *afraid* to drive. In my first year in London, I pulled out of a parking space without signaling and crashed into a taxi. Luckily the cab was covered by insurance, which took care of the damages. But I could never forget what the judge told me the day I appeared in court.

"Young lady, I beg you not to drive in this country anymore."

I gave the judge my word and never drove again in England. I guess I was still keeping my word in America, hoping I would never have to drive in Los Angeles either. But that became almost impossible.

Misha had a huge old Cadillac with a manual transmission.

Its air conditioner did not work. I still remember the day we used it to deliver a huge basket of flowers to a funeral.

The son of the deceased had personally come to the shop to place the order and asked us to put an eight-by-ten-inch photo of his dead father in the middle of the basket. After a round of negotiations he agreed to pay $150 dollars for the basket and delivery. The amount paid for the order barely covered our costs, but we were determined to make a name for our shop.

Kian was afraid of the picture of the dead father and begged me to hide it somewhere until the basket was ready to go. But she did a great job designing the royal-looking arrangement. We planted the picture of the deceased in the middle of the basket, and Misha and I went off in her Cadillac to deliver it.

It was a hot summer day. Misha was driving, and I was in the front seat with the map in my right hand and holding the basket of flowers with my left hand with all of the windows open. We were both new in town and had no idea how big the city truly was. The hot air blowing in felt like the heat of a hair dryer. We were wilting and so were the flowers. Getting lost for almost an hour on highway 101, we didn't arrive at the funeral in North Hollywood until the mourners were leaving.

The two of us carried the basket of dying flowers inside. We kept pushing through the crowd in the opposite direction, as though we were on time. Someone finally told us that the funeral was over. Still, we placed the flowers in the church.

Sadly, the more we tried, the less we achieved. Our shop was too small and so was our refrigerator. Our Iranian friends had done their best to recommend us, but we were barely known in the neighborhood, and the money I had put aside for a rainy day was thinning.

———

MY FRIEND HOUSHANG Touzie had just finished working on a movie, *Into the Night*, with Michelle Pfeiffer and Jeff Goldblum, portraying a backgammon club owner. He had also staged his first play written in exile, *All the Sons of Lady Iran*, with the help of an excellent cast.

I went to see his play. It was performed at the Lincoln Auditorium in Santa Monica, and it blew my mind. The audience laughed and cried throughout, and when it was over they gave him a long standing ovation. Houshang's sociopolitical observations of his new environment were sharp, deep, courageous, and funny.

He was so surprised to see me. I told him how much I enjoyed the play and invited him to visit the flower shop. He could not believe that I had actually started my own business in such a short period of time.

Houshang was going to leave soon to tour Canada, but he asked me to read his latest play, *Café Nostalgia*, to see if I could envision myself in it.

In the play, Café Nostalgia is owned by an Iranian couple, an ex-history teacher named Mr. Akbar and his wife, Afagh. I was developing quite a crush on the devilishly handsome Houshang and I was more than eager to read it.

I devoured it in one night. My proposed part, Afagh, was a symbolic portrayal of every strong Iranian woman, someone who simply refuses to give up. She loves her Iranian heritage but is not as nostalgic about it as her husband, who would be played by Hassan Khayatbashi, a popular Iranian TV star.

Houshang and I met again, and I slyly told him how much I enjoyed reading his play and how eager I was to work on it. He said that he had already talked to a couple of Iranian actors in Los Angeles and wanted me to start rehearsals with them as soon as possible while he went on the road for three weeks in Canada. I was thrilled. I would close the shop at six in the evening and start rehearsals at seven. We would work for a couple of hours at my place every night.

Houshang called a few times from Canada, and I was excited to speak with him each time.

My roommate was the happiest one of all, because she had found a great excuse to "celebrate" every night. I got home early one afternoon just as an ambulance pulled over and three young men jumped out, running toward my building. I opened the door for them, and they asked me where the elevator was. I told them to follow me. We got into the elevator and I inquired which floor they were going to. They said, "Number two-one-three." I thought, Oh, okay, they are going to . . . what?

"Did you say two-one-three?" I asked.

They said yes.

"That is my apartment. What is happening?"

"There's the possibility of an overdose," they said.

"An overdose, of what, and who?"

"Cocaine overdose, a young man," they said.

We got out of the elevator and ran to my apartment. My roommate's boyfriend, a tall and heavy young man, was lying very still on the floor, and my roommate was crying. The paramedics examined him to make sure that none of his bones were broken from his collapse on the floor. They kept asking him questions such as "What is your name? What is today's date? What year is it? What is the name of the president of the United States?"

The poor man could barely respond. Finally the three paramedics put him on a stretcher and took him to the hospital.

I was shocked and speechless. I was aware of Mimi's cocaine use but stupidly thought that she used it only occasionally. Besides, I do not like to poke my nose in other people's business. It was not for me to tell her what to do. I was her roommate, not her mother. But the bigger problem was that she was two months behind in the rent and kept telling me that her brother in France would be sending her money.

That night I decided to move out and get a studio apartment in the same building. Enough is enough, I thought. I needed a place of my own, never mind how small.

HOUSHANG RETURNED FROM Canada, and we started rehearsing extensively, every night, at a huge studio in the Valley. I had asked Misha to take care of the shop while I was working on the play. She did her best. I would sometimes go to the shop in the late afternoons to see how it was doing and have dinner with Misha or my other friends at Deezzy next door. The owner had designed it like a Persian teahouse and decorated it with posters of Persian paintings and calligraphies, neatly framed in wood. It even had a small stage where Iranian musicians played nostalgic melodies and sometimes hosted great Iranian singers. One night I sat with my coworkers from the flower shop, enjoying the atmosphere and each other's company.

I saw Houshang. He was sitting with a girl, his friend Ali, and Ali's girlfriend. On my way out I decided to stop by their table to say hello and overheard the girl next to him saying

" . . . and who the hell does she think she is?" Houshang replied, "Shohreh Aghdashloo," just as I arrived at their table.

Houshang got up and introduced me to the people at the table but I was not looking at them at all. I ignored the offender completely and would not even make eye contact. I let Houshang finish the introductions then whispered to him that I was tired and was going home. He bent down to kiss my cheeks, but I turned my face and kissed his lips. Houshang was paralyzed. He is a shy and private man. I guess he could not believe what was happening.

I turned around and left, but I heard a commotion on my way out, and my friends told me to look back. Houshang was sitting on his chair, soaked in soda, his lips red with my Chanel lipstick. Apparently his date had poured a large glass of Coke on his head.

Houshang did not mention it at our rehearsal the next day, and neither did I. But something had changed between us.

One night Houshang was driving me home after a long rehearsal. We stopped at a gas station and he asked me if I cared for an ice cream.

"Ice cream?" I said. "At this time of the night? At a gas station?"

'This is America, Shohreh, anything is possible. You can have ice cream anytime you feel like it. And I happen to love their machine-produced vanilla ice cream."

I said I would have one. When he got back to the car he offered me the cone through the window. But as I extended my hand, he asked me a question.

"Will you marry me?" he said.

I paused then said, "Yes."

"When would you like to get married?" he asked.

"Anytime," I replied.

"How about now?"

"Now? At this time of night? How is it possible?"

"This is America, Shohreh, anything is possible, just say yes and you will see how easy it is."

"What are we waiting for?" I said.

He jumped in the car, drove to a liquor store, and asked me what my favorite drink was.

"Grand Marnier," I said.

He asked me to wait in the car. As I was sitting there in the dark, watching the store, I wondered if I was doing the right thing. I loved being with him. His presence gave me a certain kind of happiness and peacefulness that I had once shared with Aydin.

He returned to the car after a few minutes with the smallest bottle of Grand Marnier I had ever seen in my life, and then started driving again.

Years later, he told me that he could not remember the name of my favorite, fancy drink at the gas station.

"Can I have a Grand Mareee . . . ?" Houshang asked the cashier.

"You mean Grand Marnier?" replied the cashier.

"Oh, yes, Grand . . . whatever it is," said Houshang.

"Did the lady ask for it?" the cashier inquired.

"Yes, she did," said Houshang, embarrassed.

"The lady has class," said the cashier.

We drove to the airport, intent on flying to Las Vegas and finding a chapel to make our love official.

26

HIGH ROLLERS

T HE NUMBER OF night travelers at LAX, Los Angeles's main airport, was astonishing. But when we arrived in Las Vegas, it was even more alive and exciting. It was as though everyone came out at night. Some were glued to the slot machines, which were also installed at the Las Vegas airport. I simply couldn't believe that—gambling at the airport! At the casinos, others anxiously watched their friends or relatives, fearing the worst with each roll of the dice. Yet they all coexisted in harmony, dancing to the tune of the night and the never-ending ring of the slot machines.

Houshang asked the cabdriver to take us to a chapel where we could get married. He took us to a beautiful white and pink miniature chapel on Las Vegas Boulevard. Its chamber was covered in white lace and white baskets of pink flowers on tall white stands against the walls. The priest's Russian-American assistant put our name down on the list. We stood in a long line of people who were also about to get married.

When we were finally standing in the presence of the priest, we were asked if we had any witnesses. We said we did not. The young priest called for Jack and Jill, the chapel's house witnesses, to come forward. I wished I was dressed more appropriately for my wedding. I was in my jeans and an argyle shirt. We were then sworn to love each other for all eternity, for better or worse, till death do us part. Houshang was asked to kiss the bride. Being the shy man that he is, he kissed me on the cheeks and whispered in my ears that he would kiss me more affectionately when we were not in public.

We spent the night at the Caesars Palace on the Strip, Las Vegas's version of ancient Rome, in paradise—Nevada, U.S.A. We walked through its ornate lobby, admiring its classical architecture, polished marble floors, and exquisite lamp reproductions, all theatrically lit. We strolled down the plush carpet leading to the casino. Houshang loved to play roulette. I asked him how much he wanted to risk, and he replied, "A hundred dollars."

My lucky number has always been nineteen since I won a fortune for a dear friend in Monaco during my time as a student in London. A couple of my fellow students, rich kids, had decided to visit the South of France and took me with them. We were in the classic Monte Carlo Casino, and my friends kept losing their pocket money. By around two in the morning, they had lost all the cash they had brought with them except for a few hundred francs, about $250. It seemed like we would have to shorten the trip and head back to London, so I asked them to allow me to put all their cash on one number. They did and I randomly chose number 19, as it had been the best year of my life. Before the night was over we'd won a couple of thousand dollars.

What I was hoping for now was to win on my lucky number in Vegas, too. But before we knew it, the little marble was sitting on number 9. Well, I was half right!

My new husband looked at me in despair and said that he had hoped to play for at least an hour with the hundred. I told him he did not have to waste a minute if Lady Luck was on his side. "Put it all on one number and get it over with," I said. We went back to our rather tacky faux Roman room and made passionate love not only for the first time but also as husband and wife. I was so happy for this new beginning.

The Grand Marnier took its toll the following morning. I woke up with a horrible headache and to the loud sound of young tourists splashing and laughing in the large pool. The sun was shining at its fullest, penetrating the loose seams of the closed curtains. I did a double take when I woke up. I turned to my left first and saw Houshang waking up next to me. Then I turned to my right and saw a piece of paper, neatly rolled in a pink ribbon and a bow. It looked very much like a diploma handed out on graduation day. It was our marriage certificate issued at the chapel. Realizing I was actually married to my best friend, whom I dearly loved, I decided I was blessed to have found a partner who had similar dreams to my own. We both aspired to become successful and make our lives meaningful by doing something significant. We admired the arts, loved poetry, and lived for the theater. Houshang was not only a great artist; he was also a handsome, kindhearted man. And of course the sexual tension between us was palpable.

Obviously the plain ceremony at the chapel had nothing in common with my first wedding, so elaborately celebrated back in Iran. I loved the straightforwardness of it all, and its simplicity.

We hurriedly left the hotel to get back in time for our evening rehearsal in Los Angeles. We jumped into a cab and were heading to the airport when I realized I had left my jewelry from Iran back at the hotel. I was distraught. Houshang looked at me as if to say "I told you so." Then he told me he'd packed it for me. To this day, he still searches our hotel rooms thoroughly before we check out.

I ASKED HOUSHANG to move in with me, now that I had my own apartment. He was living with his brother at the time and gladly accepted the offer. But we did not tell a soul that we were married, not even our families. We had a show to put on and did not want our marriage to take center stage.

I would go to the flower shop every morning, rehearse in the afternoons, and share my American dreams with Houshang at night: dreams of children, owning a home together, and living and working in a peaceful environment.

To our dismay the Iranian American magazine *Javanan* had found out about our elopement to Las Vegas through their sources and published the news. Our colleagues wondered if it was true. We told them the magazine had it wrong but that we would get married in due time and invite all of them to our wedding.

"We must concentrate on the play first," said Houshang.

EARLY ONE MORNING, not long after our return from Vegas, I woke up to the piercing sound of the telephone next to our bed. It was my friend and former host Ian, calling from London. He was going to Aspen with his siblings and was wondering if I would like to join them the following weekend. I gladly accepted and hung up, still sleepy with my eyes closed.

I did not ski. Ashur, my favorite stage director, once told me, "A serious actor does not get herself involved with a sport that may cause serious injuries."

But I was in need of a vacation. It would be nice to take three days off from all the stress of rehearsing the play and breathing life into the penniless flower shop.

Then I heard Houshang's voice. He asked me who I was talking to. I opened my eyes and turned around and told him who it was and that I needed a short break. He immediately jumped out of bed. He was furious with me for accepting the invitation. He said I should have asked him first, not only as my husband but also as my director. He said I needed his permission to leave.

I could not believe my ears! I said, "But I will come back refreshed and will be even more useful."

He said no, and I became angry.

I got up and went to my desk. I picked up our marriage certificate and tore it into pieces. I told him that he was out of his mind if he thought he could take away my freedom with a piece of paper issued in Vegas.

He was speechless. I put on a dress and dashed out of our apartment. He followed me all the way to the flower shop. Misha was already there. Houshang hesitated at the door and then left. He called me a couple of hours later and asked me to let him explain himself.

I did. When I got home, I saw him with the pieces of our marriage certificate glued back together. We laughed, and he told me how sorry he was. He said I had hurt his feelings by ignoring him and not inviting him to go with me. He said I could have discussed it with him first and that he was hurt because he, too, needed a short break.

Still, what else could I do? He had not been invited, and I had not even told my friend I was married. I was dead asleep when Ian called and all I had heard was the word *vacation*. I apologized for my behavior and told Houshang I had decided not to go to Aspen. I would not have enjoyed the trip knowing he would be hurt.

IN SEPTEMBER 1987, the play *Café Nostalgia* ran for four consecutive nights at the Lincoln Auditorium in Santa Monica. Its premiere was more than promising. All six hundred tickets were sold out. Iranian stores on Westwood and in Santa Monica displayed our posters and sold our tickets.

I went to the stores to collect the money and brought back several thousand dollars in cash in my shoulder bag. I could not wait to get home and pour the entire sack of cash on the bed, just like they do in the movies. I'd always wanted to do it and see how it would feel. I stretched my hands as high up as possible and poured all the money on the bed in slow motion. The bills floated out of the bag and danced in the air as they landed on the bed one by one.

Houshang was watching me, smiling. "You had to do it, didn't you?"

"Yes," I said, throwing the empty bag aside.

We stood there in each other's arms, in our tiny studio apartment, watching our American Dream coming true, realizing we had a built-in audience who enjoyed our work and would come to see us wherever we performed. It was this core audience's unflinching support that would eventually bring me to the Oscars.

HOUSHANG ASKED ME to marry him again—now that I had torn apart our marriage certificate. I agreed.

We went to City Hall a couple of days later and again waited in a long line. It was time to invite our close friends to a nice restaurant and celebrate our new official marriage.

I called my parents in Tehran. By now both my parents were in their late fifties. My father had retired from the Ministry of Health as managing director. I also phoned Shahram in London and invited him to our party. My middle brother, Shahriar, was still in Tehran practicing medicine, and Shahrokh, who believed in being an ordinary citizen, was an engineer. Unfortunately, the ones in Iran would have faced difficulties obtaining quick visas to America. But everyone was thrilled to hear the news. They wished me a long and happy marriage. I begged them to come and visit us as soon as they could. My mother promised me she would come over and that she would bring my father if I gave them a grandchild. They already had two by my brother Shahriar, but they wanted to see my children.

Houshang called his parents and was surprised to discover that they were coming to visit their sons in America. I did not know Houshang's parents but had heard a lot about them. Houshang loved his mother and had told me how she had devoted her life to raising him and his five siblings. His father, on the other hand, was a man of leisure, an incredibly good-looking rich man who had lost a fortune partying and gambling when he was young, but was still loved by his wife.

Houshang's mother cried on the phone and told him that she wanted us to have a real wedding. But we could barely get by financially, let alone throw a big wedding party—especially an Iranian wedding party with the traditional five-course meal, tons of sweets and fruits, flowers, live band, a wedding dress, and an expensive suit. Neither of us had a permanent job. Wasting our savings on a wedding like that sounded overly indulgent. I was at a loss for words when Houshang told me about his mom's wish. How could I not agree with her? She was an Iranian mother and had every right to ask for an Iranian wedding. But how could we fulfill her wish?

I was at the flower shop, thinking of how to solve such a delicate matter, when the Iranian designer Pari Malek called. I had met Malek at a fashion show years before the revolution but never had the pleasure of working with her. Her voice took me back to years earlier when I was just sixteen.

Malek told me she had read the recent news in *Javanan* magazine that I was getting married in California and was wondering if it was true. I told her that it was. She asked me if we were going to have a party, and I said, "We may." She then asked to dress me for the wedding, and I gladly accepted.

I called Club 44, a charming disco restaurant in Glendale. It was the nest for newly immigrated Iranians who feasted on the club's Persian cuisine and danced to popular Iranian songs. Iranians from all backgrounds came to celebrate their freedom, to listen to nostalgic songs, and to watch their favorite singers performing live with the club's band on the weekends.

The club was owned by two Armenian-Iranian brothers. They were more than happy to let us use the place for free. I could not believe it. I insisted on paying, but they said that throwing our wedding party there would be a great advertisement for the club. They also offered the band for free and only asked us to pay for the food and labor, charging twelve dollars per person. Their generosity was amazing.

We made a list of our family and friends, which had 120 names on it. The wedding was on.

I called Shahla, my friend from Iran, who was now living in San Francisco, and gave her the news. She was very happy and told me that she wanted to do something for us. She said she would take care of the fruits and desserts, including the wedding cake. Houshang's best man, Farhad, provided us with a large number of alcoholic and nonalcoholic beverages. The club removed its own liquor from the bar and replaced it with ours.

Houshang and I woke up at five o'clock in the morning on the day of our wedding to purchase fresh flowers at the market and take them to my flower shop, where Misha and Kian would start designing the bride's bouquet and the centerpieces. Our ride to the party was a gift from Masha, another friend of Houshang's, who was working with a limousine company at the time.

I was happy but also felt sad. I wished my parents were with me. In fact, I choked up with sorrow when the small ceremony, conducted by a marriage registrar, began. I held my tears back and tried my best not to cry, or to make the guests sad.

Mr. Shahbaz, the marriage registrar, first recited some of Hafez's great poetry to us. He then talked at length about the responsibilities of marriage and finally asked us the imperative, universal question.

"Do you, Houshang, take Shohreh as your beloved wife, in sickness and in health . . ."

Almost two hundred people showed up at our wedding, even though we had invited far fewer. But friends who had found out about it decided to surprise us, including some prominent Iranian singers who honored us with wedding songs.

We had a blast. Houshang's mom was the happiest one of all. The sweet lady sat next to the dancing area all night, watching the crowd dance to Persian songs. She liked me and genuinely believed that I was a great match for her son.

I danced all night. Our friend Kouros filmed the wedding. In Iran, my mother had purchased a bootlegged tape of our wedding, shot by a guest, and called me after watching it. She said I should have let others dance more, meaning I should not have danced so much. I said, "But it was my night, Mom."

The party went on until 3:00 A.M. Our guests were having such a good time they almost refused to leave. The last singer of the night asked the guests jokingly to leave us alone and let us go home as husband and wife.

Masha took us home, with our tired legs stretched out in the limo.

We got home at five in the morning. We had not had a chance to rest for almost twenty-four hours. It took me a few minutes to get out of Malek's beaded wedding dress and its long train. I hung it properly in its cover, ready to be returned to the designer later. I spent another couple of minutes pulling out all the clips in my hair. My hair and makeup were a gift from another friend of mine, Ahmed, who owned a hair salon in Beverly Hills. I felt like Cinderella, after the stroke of twelve had already passed.

The carriage had turned into a pumpkin. The horses were turned to mice. The long elaborate gown was gone, and I was now in my pajamas. But I was married to my Prince Charming.

27

THE POLITICAL DIVIDE

WHILE WE WERE getting married in L.A., Akbar Rafsanjani was about to become the president of Iran, while the Ayatollah Khomeini was elevated to the country's supreme leader. Rafsanjani was a hard-liner who believed in the same principles as the Ayatollah. He is still considered the wealthiest man in the country, worth over a billion dollars. He had started as an owner of pistachio plantations, but when he came to power he expanded his empire significantly with Iranian oil. The youth of Iran felt betrayed. A revolution that was meant to bring freedom brought only fear and religious tyranny. *Hijabs* had become mandatory for women from the age of nine and up.

HOUSHANG AND I had to postpone our national tour with *Café Nostalgia* when we were offered roles together in the feature film *Guests of Hotel Astoria*, produced by a studio company in

Holland. I loved the plot: a dozen unjustly persecuted Iranians are smuggled by bus to Istanbul. They are marooned there, living in the run-down Hotel Astoria, all awaiting visas or political asylum from the U.S. and European embassies.

Guests of Hotel Astoria exposed the plight of thousands of Iranians who were emigrating abroad, using Istanbul as their first entry gate into the free world. If they were rejected by their designated embassies, they were trapped.

The producer's financial offer was not exactly what I had in mind, but the message of the film was worthy. It shed light on the injustices in Iran under the Islamic Republic and accurately portrayed the devastating situation of the destitute illegal Iranian immigrants in Turkey.

The film was to be shot in Los Angeles, LaGuardia Airport in New York, Amsterdam Airport, and finally in Istanbul and its airport. Filming began in early 1988. I was torn between my love for acting and my duty to my business partner, Misha. Our flower shop had taken a turn for the worse and was not doing well at all. Houshang and I had spent a substantial portion of our savings from our theatrical income to try to save the shop, but it wasn't going to be enough.

I went to the Pot Lady and told Misha the hard truth. I explained to her that I had opened the shop for a little income while I pursued my acting career. I had now come to the point where I could no longer keep up with the shop's demands and its financial shortages. I told her I would be more than happy to give her my half and sign the shop entirely over to her. She accepted my offer, though I left the Pot Lady feeling horrible. But my love for acting was in my soul.

IT WAS DURING this time that I started developing a strange physical ailment. I had a series of attacks, where my heart fluttered out of control and left me feeling like I had been terribly beaten. I was no longer able to focus on my work and could not stand being in a crowd. I had no idea why this was happening to me.

Nevertheless, I had to appear at a luncheon at the Beverly Hills Hotel, given by the Society of Iranian Women in L.A. I was mortified as I looked at the audience and delivered my speech, my heart pounding. I managed to get through it, rushing to the bathroom to have my attack there afterward.

My old friend Jaleh had come back to America and was now living in L.A. We ran into each other at the luncheon after having lost contact for years. Jaleh joined me in the bathroom and asked me what was wrong. I told her, and she took me home. She found me a psychiatrist the day after and pleaded for an urgent appointment.

Due to his hectic daily schedule, the doctor saw me at nine o'clock the following evening. He asked me how it had all started. I told him that I was having lunch with the producer of my film in his backyard, discussing the characters in the film. I was admiring the producer's dog, a four-year-old German shepherd who looked like my dog, Pasha, back in Iran. Then, all of a sudden, my heart started to pound faster and faster, my palms were wet with sweat, and I thought I was going to die.

After I explained my story, the doctor asked, "What in your opinion made you overcome your fear?"

"Vivien Leigh," I said. "I was suddenly reminded of Scarlett O'Hara's fearlessness, courage, and perseverance."

The doctor asked me to tell him about my childhood and my family. It took me less than an hour to sum it up. He then told me that I was suffering from panic attacks. He said panic attacks are rooted in a deep feeling of insecurity, derived from a variety of reasons, but mostly from one's competitive and hectic lifestyle in big cities with heavy traffic.

He said I was unconsciously afraid of not being able to achieve my goals and pursue my dream. He said such attacks pull one back, like in a time tunnel, and make you compare the safe, sound, and tranquil moments of your past with the upheaval in your current life. Thinking of that time of serenity, the comparison forces you to feel frightened of the present.

He said the German shepherd had triggered it, a rush of sweet and bitter memories of the past. It took me back to the days I was happily living in my birth country, proud to witness Iran's progress. He said that I missed my father and the serenity of life under his protection. Apparently I had mentioned my father's name more than twenty times in less than an hour.

The doctor said I was the only one who could help me, by being rational and understanding, and that I should always remember that millions of people were suffering from the same illness in America.

"First, look for the trigger when the attack happens. Find out what similar objects or words draw you to the peaceful moment of your past. Second, always carry a small brown paper bag and exhale into it when the attack starts. Third, and most importantly, keep reminding yourself that you will not die. This is mental, not physical," said the doctor.

He said he would put me on a tranquilizer, but he expected me to get off of the pills as soon as I felt better and to try to manage my life without them.

"Think of your friends Vivien and Scarlett, together. You can do it."

I was given some tranquilizers to calm me down, but the pills made me feel like a tired elephant, wanting to sleep all the time.

I had to leave early for the first day of blocking the film, and I was suffering from severe fatigue. Poor Houshang was extremely worried for me, and I could see how scared he was. None of us knew anything about this mental disease, and we were afraid of it.

Krishnamurti, the great Indian philosopher, believed that the worst and truest fear is the fear of the unknown. I could not agree with him more, having experienced the fear of the unknown during the early stages of my panic attacks. I could not sleep at night. A part of me wanted to give up, retire from acting, choose a much simpler life, and live in a small town. I no longer dreamed of living on an estate like Tara.

Part of me knew Houshang would have gone along with it, wanting only for me to get well. But another part was telling me that I should not submit to these new ideas, that I should show some courage. I had come a long way in what I believed to be my passion in life. I had almost made it now, and there was no way I was turning back.

I went to rehearsal and dealt with the attacks one day at a time, following the doctor's instructions. I was constantly talking to myself, reminding myself that the illness in my head was illusory. I thought I ought to be able to overcome it, knowing the cause. I managed to finish my work with just a few interruptions. I had not yet fully recovered, but I was committed to making a film that portrayed people like me in a far worse situation. *Who was I to complain?*

Houshang and I went to New York and joined the rest of the cast, whose scenes took place there, including Ashur, the avant-garde director I used to work with at the workshop in Iran. He was now living in New York.

We were all happy to see one another again and to be able to work together on such a meaningful project. We went right to a modest Italian restaurant in the city and talked all night. It was our first gathering after eight years apart. The owner of the restaurant found out that we were a couple of artists from Iran and sent us a bottle of wine. He let us talk loudly while discussing politics long into the night. None of us could believe what was happening back home.

The end of the Iran-Iraq war had a huge impact on the people of my homeland, who had not seen the face of war for generations. Ordinary citizens were scattered, scared, and exhausted. The nonconformists had created a life underground that not only allowed them to escape the Iraqi bombs but also to avoid the regime's brutal law enforcers, called SAVAMA—the new and more brutal version of SAVAK. Because of SAVAMA, Evin Prison had to expand its area for "political prisoners."

THE SHOOTING OF the film started again the next day at La-Guardia. We were all exhausted and looked tired, but I was fine with my appearance, since I was supposed to portray a drained-looking woman who is seven months pregnant and terrified after having entered the U.S.A. under a false passport. Since our permit to shoot at the airport was good only for one night, and the production had already cost the producers tens of thousands of dollars, we worked long into the night.

We went back to our hotel at three in the morning, and I packed for the trip to Istanbul the following evening. I sat on the edge of the bed and looked at the hypnotic view of New York City: sleek modern skyscrapers next to buildings in an old-European style of architecture. All were illuminated by thousands of glistening lights. It was a living tableau of the past, the present, and the future.

Houshang sat next to me and asked me if I was all right. I told him I was thinking of the woman I portrayed in the movie and felt sad that she had no one to go to once she landed in the United States. He hugged me and told me that I had him. He then asked me if I wanted to rehearse our romantic kiss in the movie.

I reminded him the scene had already been shot, but still I could use a good kiss. I needed to reconnect with our love, passion, and humanity. It was time to kiss and care for each other and make love.

Houshang was not needed for filming in Istanbul and was not going with us any further. It was the first time Houshang and I would be apart since our marriage, and we both looked lost when kissing each other good-bye. He was going to join me in Germany after the shooting was done, to start our theatrical tour of *Café Nostalgia* in Frankfurt.

MY COLLEAGUE MOHSEN and I flew to Istanbul, where I had asked my parents to join me. (Turkey never closed its borders to Iranians even during the revolution and the war.) We had not seen each other since their last visit to London, three years before, and I missed them deeply. It is not easy to live so far away from your loved ones. My mother looked almost the same, but my father had gotten older. The poor man hated the regime and what it was doing to the people of Iran. They were so happy to see me, and I was on cloud nine having them there. I even asked them to play the part of the two pedestrians in one of my scenes, and they agreed to it gladly.

The two weeks in Istanbul with my parents made me feel much better, but I was still suffering from panic attacks and kept fighting them off by trying to understand their roots.

Though we'd started filming already, the Turkish authorities had not yet granted us permission to shoot at Istanbul Airport. But the assistant director decided to go ahead and shoot the scene according to the schedule, regardless of what the authorities might say or do.

Mohsen and I got to the airport in the early morning and joined the crew laying their equipment out by the only entrance to the airport. The cinematographer was stepping behind the camera when a policeman asked him if we had a permit to shoot. He said we did. The policeman did not ask to see it and instead suggested that we use real people in the background. Our cameraman looked at us and said, "What are we waiting for?" Mohsen and I joined the actual crowd at the entrance while the extras waited in the parking lot.

In this scene, the two characters are trying to fly to the

Netherlands with false passports. This is their first attempt to flee Istanbul and join family in Amsterdam. The irony was that most of the Iranian passengers who were flying out of Istanbul that day shared common stories with the characters of our movie. Many had fled Iran and were lucky enough to get a visa to America. I was having an emotional breakdown that day. I wanted to be back in America and I felt such compassion for those who hoped fate would take them there as well.

My tongue felt like a piece of dried wood in my mouth, and my heart was in my throat. I still do not know how I managed to work twelve hours that day. I wished Houshang was with me. He could have helped me. But I had to overcome the fear myself.

We were almost done with the interior shots when a high-ranking Turkish general entered the airport and became angry at what he saw. He couldn't believe two actual policemen had volunteered to be in the film. The general asked them what the hell they were doing, posing in front of a camera while on duty. They said they were just trying to help us by portraying policemen in our film.

The general shouted, "You are not actors! You are peasants! You are supposed to be policemen, you idiots!"

MY PARENTS AND I celebrated our last night together at a Turkish cabaret, listening to the beautiful voices of its regional singers and feasting on Turkish food. My mother was surprised by how little I ate. She said I might be pregnant. I asked her why she thought so, and she said, "Because you have lost color and have eaten too little." She did not know anything about my panic attacks, and I did not intend to tell her.

My heart sank when my parents left. I wondered when I would see them again. They were getting old and I was their first child. They had given my brothers and me a great life, and had done their best to take good care of us. I could not be there for them now, and take care of them in return. I wished I was rich and could get them out of Iran. I yearned to provide them a decent life abroad. But I could not. My father would not have accepted it even if I could. He was a proud man and would always stay in Iran.

I took my parents to the airport the next day and watched them disappear behind the entry doors. Then I leaned against a handrail on the curbside and cried, cursing the political divide that had separated us from each other.

NEXT UP WAS Amsterdam, where the last piece of the movie was to be shot. This time we did have a proper permit to film, and the airport authorities did their best to accommodate us.

During a break, I was asked by the airport immigration police if I would talk to an Iranian passenger who did not speak a word of English, or any other language except Farsi. They did not have a Farsi-speaking translator on hand and were wondering if I could help them.

Two policemen took me to where the Iranian woman was waiting for a miracle to happen. I saw a young pregnant woman in her early thirties with her five-year-old son clutching his mother's skirt. It was as though my character had jumped out of the film and was facing me in real life.

I explained to the young woman that the police wanted to know which country she flew from, and why she did not have a passport. She was shaking, and her son was crying. The child was hungry. I asked the police if we could give them some food from the film's craft services, and it was soon delivered to us. The poor kid took a large bite out of his ham sandwich and gulped it down with a Coca-Cola. He wouldn't take his teary and puffy eyes off of his mother.

She then started to whisper to me in Farsi: "Please do not tell them this. I tore my Iranian passport into pieces and flushed it down the toilet on the plane. I was smuggled into Pakistan. The opposition helped me. They gave me some money, and I bought a fake Pakistani passport and a fake visa to Holland to get on the plane. I am coming from Pakistan now. But please do not tell them what I told you or I will be deported to Iran."

She was told by her opposition friends that the authorities in Holland would not deport her as long as she did not have a travel document on her that indicated her country of origin. She told me that her husband had been a member of an Iranian opposition called the Mujahideen Khalq. It was the Islamic Republic's most infamous opposition group. The mujahideen believed they were engaged in a long-term guerrilla war against the Islamic Republic. Her husband had been executed at Tehran's Evin Prison shortly after being captured at their home. She said she would be killed, too, if she went back to Iran, for she was a member of the group as well. I was speechless, and knew she was right. Hundreds of mujahideen, mostly young people, men and women, had been tortured, raped, and killed in prison.

Women of Iran were deprived of their basic rights. Many had been jailed, tortured, raped, and hanged for being members of ethnic or religious minorities or being involved in political activities.

Mona, a sixteen-year-old Baha'i girl, was hanged in July 1984 for refusing to conform and sign a petition for mercy, in which she would denounce her birth religion, the Baha'i faith, and convert to Islam. Her tragic death made a huge impact on concerned citizens all over the world.

In 1985, the United Nations' special representatives to Iran began issuing regular reports documenting allegations of sexual violence and rape in Iran's prisons. A 1987 report noted that six sympathizers of Iran's mujahideen testified about experiencing and witnessing many forms of torture. One woman, Mina Vatani, reported that she witnessed seventy people being executed in Evin Prison in early 1982, and that the victims included a pregnant woman and women who had been raped.

In 1988, the same year we were filming *Hotel Astoria*, representatives held informal hearings at which sixteen former prisoners testified about their experiences in prison, which included torture and rape. Seven were Baha'is and nine described themselves as sympathizers of the mujahideen. One witness testified that a woman in her sixties had been raped and executed; another stated that she witnessed Revolutionary Guards raping young girls.

I was torn between the truth, risking the woman's life, my conscience, and my responsibility as a translator. Then I remembered what my old friend Shamim once taught me.

He had been at our place in Tehran when my first husband and I were arguing over something. I turned to Shamim and asked him who was right. He said my husband was right. I looked at him in disbelief and said I thought he was a fair-minded intellectual. I asked him, "What would you stand by, the truth or your friend?"

He said he would stand by his friend regardless of the truth.

I knew the woman was going to be killed if deported to Iran. So I gathered all my strength and stood by her.

I told the policemen that she refused to tell me the truth and that I did not understand a word she said, as she spoke a different dialect of Farsi. I never knew what happened to her, but I heard from the policeman who escorted me back to the set that she was going to be taken to the city of Amsterdam for further inquiry.

I hoped she was able to obtain political asylum without having a passport. I wished she could stay in the Netherlands, that peaceful country and beautiful land of magnificent tulips. Its democratic law would treat her as a human being and give her child a chance to grow up in a civil society, where his mother would not be tortured, raped, and hanged for having a different ideology.

I left Holland as soon as possible and joined Houshang in Germany.

28

CARAVAN

HOUSHANG HAD ALREADY flown to Munich to start rehearsing with our new *Café Nostalgia* cast in Germany. I was thrilled to see him and hugged the poor man nearly to death. I was so glad to be with my best friend and lover once again.

Taking our own theatrical group would have been a lot easier for us, but the high cost of flying them to Europe and providing their accommodations forced us instead to use local Iranian actors in each country where we performed. Many of them had been well-known actors in Iran who were now working in menial jobs. We were more than willing not only to give them a chance to act again but also to participate in a Farsi-speaking play that aimed to keep the lights of the Iranian theater on in exile.

Houshang and I were offered the opportunity to stay with

our sponsor and his wife, and we gladly accepted, knowing the hotel prices in Munich. Our sponsor called himself Mark, and he and his wife and their oddly large parrot, Fraulein, lived in a tiny two-bedroom apartment, perhaps a little more than a thousand square feet. Our room was next to the living room, where the yellow and turquoise parrot sat on top of her cage all day, constantly whistling and reciting bits of verses of Persian poems. His favorite word was *khoshgeleh*, which means "beautiful," and he kept repeating it every time he saw me. Our sponsor was proud of his parrot and loved him to death.

I, on the other hand, could not stand any kind of animal with feathers. I had once been attacked by a fighter rooster on one of my childhood trips to a village and was afraid of birds in general, let alone a parrot half my size. Our sponsor assured me that his parrot was extremely gentle. But I was not sure if it was me or my environment that was making me feel so drained and vulnerable.

EIGHT HUNDRED SEATS were in the theater, and all were occupied by the Iranian audience who came to see the play. They laughed and cried and cheered. Houshang and I were thrilled to see the play thriving but were disappointed to find out that our sponsor was not honest with us. He was claiming a lot of expenses, such as the cost of building the set. He added all these imaginary numbers on a scrap of paper and handed it to us with no receipts. He then deducted the expenses from the revenue and gave us what was left, which hardly covered our performers' wages. We decided not to argue. We should have asked for a legal contract but we had not.

Our next performance was in a theater in Frankfurt, with five hundred red velvet seats before us. Our new local sponsor was a proud man and was truly glad to have us. This time we signed a contract. We performed two nights in a row, and hundreds of Iranians came to see *Café Nostalgia*. Our audiences encouraged us to return soon, with their standing ovations after each performance.

I should have been pleased to have achieved so much in such little time, but I was not. It was not just the panic attacks and my mind tormenting me with snapshots of the past. It was physical, too. My body ached. I felt bloated, sleepy, and tired most of the time. Suddenly I had become too sensitive and too emotional. Was it the bittersweet sense of nostalgia in the play that I lived with every night? Or was it the strong, magnetic force of love that I was receiving from the Iranian audience? I had missed being surrounded by them, and perhaps I was overwhelmed when I experienced it again.

We arrived in Cologne after seven and a half hours crushed in a small car with three others. Between the terrible roads and traffic, the ride was agony. But our last performance was as successful as all the other ones.

We had finished our tour of Germany. I had been on the road for almost two months now and was truly exhausted. All I wanted to do was go home to America. But we had promised our friends in London we would do the play there, too. There were a handful of good Iranian actors in London, and they were excited to help us stage the play.

We flew to London the next day and were greeted by our

actor friends. They were enthusiastic and ready to start the re-hearsals. My brother Shahram had graduated from Oxford University and married a beautiful, fine young lady named Sita. They invited us to stay with them, and we gladly accepted their offer. All I could think about was sleep.

29

MOOD SWINGS

MY BROTHER AND I were so happy to be together again. We played backgammon all evening and talked about our childhood days, wishing the whole family could be together again.

The rehearsals started soon, and I kept searching for an apartment to rent for a few weeks. I didn't want to overstay our welcome with my brother, who was so kind he probably would have let us stay there forever. I was still not feeling well, although the number of panic attacks had declined. I decided to see my gynecologist, Dr. Love, in London. It had been over a year since I had left the city.

She was happy to see me, and much happier to hear that I was married as she examined me and asked me questions regarding my health. Then she took off her disposable gloves, threw them in the trash can, and asked me, if it was "planned."

"If what was planned?" I asked.

"The baby," she replied.

I felt paralyzed, my mind traveling faster than light.

Suddenly it dawned on me that I had not had my period for a while. How careless of me not to pay any attention to my body! What on earth was happening to me? Then I started hearing the doctor's voice, echoing in my head: *a baby . . . a baby . . . a baby . . .*

Now I knew why I had become so vulnerable and emotional. I was carrying a baby! A seed of love that was surely sown on our final night of shooting *Guests of Hotel Astoria* in New York when Houshang and I affectionately made love in our hotel room before the panoramic view of the Chrysler Building.

I was suddenly filled with such affection. I wished immediately that it would be a girl. Ever since I had seen *Gone With the Wind*, I had promised myself that I would name my daughter Tara, after Scarlett's home. Soon after, I had read *Pride and Prejudice*, by Jane Austen, my favorite female novelist. I wanted her name to be the middle name for my future imaginary daughter, Tara-Jane.

Now that I was actually pregnant, I got to speculate about the other 50 percent chance that I would give birth to a boy, and what I would like to name him. I could name him Rhett, after the charming Mr. Butler, or perhaps Mr. Darcy, from *Pride and Prejudice*.

I did not walk to the nearby Underground station after I left the doctor's office. I floated. I could not wait to share the news with Houshang and the family. Shahram's flat was on the fourth floor of an old apartment building with no elevator. I stormed through the door and flew up the stairs like I was Mary Poppins, taking two and three steps at a time, shouting from the top of my lungs, "I'm having a baby!"

My brother heard my voice and met me at the top of the stairs.

"Did you say you are having a baby?" he asked.

I nodded because I was breathless.

"Why are you running then? You should be careful, come in."

I loved his caution and calmness at all times.

I wish you could have seen Houshang's face when I gave him the news. He was motionless, in a state of disbelief, just as I had been when I heard the good news. We immediately started talking about our future plans. I was eight weeks pregnant, and the play was set to go on the stage in two weeks, at the Polish Center. After that was a tour of the United Kingdom.

I knew I could manage to work for a while, at least as long as I could hide my swollen belly. But I could not fly home to the U.S.A. if we waited too long. Many airlines had restrictions regarding pregnant passengers in their third trimester. In the end, we decided to skip the tour in the U.K. and go home once we finished the performances in London.

I could not go to sleep that first night, dreaming of the child that was growing inside of me. I wanted the best for her, or him. I wanted it to live in a safe world, where no child is hurt, stranded, molested, or abused. I hoped my baby would live in a world in which children are all treated equally, regardless of the color of their skin or their gender. I wanted my child, if she was a girl, to live in a place where she would not be counted as half of a man legally and one quarter of a man socially in a marriage, like in the Islamic Republic of Iran, nor looked upon as only a sex object to satisfy men.

I was yearning to go back to America, but one thing that made me think twice was our health care situation. The U.K.'s health care system covered every living soul in England, including foreigners like me. Neither Houshang nor I had health insurance in the U.S.A. And now even if we did manage to get insurance, it would not have covered a "preexisting condition." Giving birth in a fairly good hospital in Los Angeles would cost at least $20,000. Giving birth in London would leave our small savings intact for our American Dream, for leasing a nice apartment, a car, and working in L.A. while raising our child. I shared my thoughts with Houshang in the morning, and once again he was speechless. He knew I was right about the health care situation. But he wanted his child to be born in America and have American citizenship. He suggested he go back to Los Angeles and see what he could do.

WE MANAGED TO find a nice studio flat close to my brother's house and kept rehearsing the play. It was successfully staged and appreciated by the Iranian audience in London, too. It received great reviews from the Iranian media in the U.K. Houshang left for the United States right after the play was over.

I did not leave my bed for two solid days. I was extremely depressed and felt weak. My sister-in-law, Sita, came to see me and asked why I did not pick up the phone. I burst into tears. She said Houshang had called them and had cried on the phone. He insisted that he wanted his child to be born in America.

I could understand his feelings but could not agree with

him, at least not until I was sure that I would not have to give birth at home, because of poverty or legal issues.

I talked to Houshang on the phone, and he promised me he would do anything to bring me back to the United States. He had decided to stay with his friend Farhad for a while until he could find a nice place for us. I needed to keep myself busy. I had to or I would have gone crazy otherwise, worrying what the future might have in store for our family.

A FRIEND OF mine had purchased a nice flat in a hip area in London and was having trouble with its interior decor. Remembering my work in Mr. K's apartment, she asked me to help her. I appreciated the offer, most of all because it forced me to get out of bed and walk around town. I visited antiques shops on Church Street off of High Street in Kensington and good old Kings Road, where my favorite crêpe shop, Astorix, was located.

I scouted out items during the week while my friend was at work then took her to purchase them on weekends. In three weeks the apartment was nearly ready. I was making plans to visit the Portobello antiques market the following weekend when Houshang called and gave me good news. He had talked to the Screen Actors Guild's health-plan department and was told that for a reasonable amount of money he could reinstate his previous health coverage, which included preexisting conditions, like a pregnant wife.

I was so happy that I started dancing all by myself. I still dance when I'm happy, but I had not done it for a while. I had missed Houshang and wanted to go home to Los Angeles. I was on my way to America before I knew it.

30

SUNNY CALIFORNIA

Houshang was still staying at his friend Farhad's place in the San Fernando Valley, a suburb of Los Angeles. It was 1988. He did not want to rent a place without me but had seen a couple of promising apartments, one of which was next door to Farhad's and was available in three weeks. The rent was a little higher than our budget allowed. But our biggest problem was that the landlord was asking for three months' rent in advance. We weren't working, and it was going to take a while for us to get back on the stage. Paying the rent with a portion of our savings was not a good idea without a Plan B.

I have always been cautious with spending my money ever since I left Iran, a practice that comes from displacement and fear of being thrown out on the street if I ever ran out. Houshang decided to take a job with a town-car service in Orange County and write his next play, *Lost in the Wind*, while awaiting passengers. The play portrays a newly immigrated young Iranian man who is desperately searching for his grandfather in Los Angeles. It was a two-act play with twenty characters in it. Mounting such a grand play seemed far-fetched without sufficient funds. But Houshang was determined to do it.

On the other hand, I was quite dysfunctional during this time. I would sleep in and then make the fifteen-minute walk to Farhad's printing shop with the help of two cans of Coca-Cola. My grandmother used to call Coca-Cola the juice of dates, her favorite fruit. She believed the soda gave her extra energy, and so do I.

Farhad tended the shop during the day and painted abstract views of nature in the evenings at home. I would sit in the shop for an hour or two and chat with Farhad while listening to the repetitive, mind-numbing noise of the printing machines. Then I would return home and wait for Houshang and Farhad to return for dinner. Houshang was working nearly twenty-hour days, still squeezing in time to write his play while waiting for his passengers.

One night I was watching television while Houshang and Farhad were discussing the rehearsal of the play. Suddenly a mild panic attack took hold of me. I was able to calm myself, but I felt a tiny stream of hot water rushing down from my belly, and spilling onto the couch. I was embarrassed and shocked. Then a sharp pain shot through my spine.

I told Houshang I thought it was time, although we were not expecting the baby for another several weeks. He paused for a second, and then grabbed the small suitcase I had already prepared for the hospital. Farhad helped me into the car, and soon I was in a room at Cedars-Sinai Hospital.

Jaleh got there in no time, and poor Houshang was torn between work and fatherhood. There was not much time left before the premiere of his play, and a lot of work was still ahead. He told me he wished to stay with me but had to leave and get on with his responsibilities as a director. He promised he would be back soon.

With Jaleh at my side, I lay in bed, anticipating the moment I had been waiting for. She encouraged me to take deep breaths and remain patient. The nurses took turns prepping me for the birth. The doctor asked if I wanted an epidural to reduce the pain, and I told him I would rather have a natural birth. I wanted to feel every second of it.

And, oh boy, did I feel every second of it! Be careful what you wish for, ladies. The real pain started after midnight, every now and then, hitting my lower back. It sped up with every centimeter I dilated. I fought to endure it with every ounce of strength in me. The battle stretched through the night.

Houshang had come back a little after midnight to see how I was doing, but I gathered all my energy and yelled at him not to enter. The poor man turned around as fast as a shooting star and waited by the door. Jaleh didn't understand why I would not allow Houshang in.

"Look at me," I said. "I am a mess. I barely recognize myself. I am roaring like a lioness. I do not want him to see me like this, and I do not want him to see me giving birth, either. This is the most private moment of a woman's life. I believe it is the only moment that I cannot share with Houshang. I do not want him to see me with my legs open wide, shouting and moaning. Maybe I'm being selfish, but I would rather not expose myself to my partner in this state of despair."

One of my girlfriends had given birth in front of her husband, and her husband could not make love to her for months afterward.

I told Jaleh, "Please tell him to come and see me when the baby is born."

Houshang reluctantly accepted my decision, but he kept coming back to the hospital to check on me. At one point, I tried to get out of bed. Jaleh asked me what I was doing, and I begged her to let me leave the hospital. "Maybe it will come if I start walking," I said.

But I could not move. I knew it was coming, and I was ready to be taken to the delivery room. My doctor was on his way. Jaleh wanted to go with me and was given a set of scrubs. But she kept complaining about the size, saying she asked for a large, but the nurse had given her small ones to embarrass her in front of the doctors.

"Are you out of your mind?" I cried. "Just put the damned things on, and let's go!"

Now in the delivery room with two nurses and Jaleh at my side, a huge round mirror hung behind the doctor, facing me. The countdown had begun, and with it the first round of futile pushes. All I could hear was "Push, push, pushhhhhhhhh!"

I gathered all my strength and pushed for the final time, realizing I should welcome the fear of the unknown this time rather than fighting it. And it came. I caught glimpses of the process in the mirror whenever the doctor bent over or reached for his tools. I saw the baby's head and I was ecstatic. I let the baby slide through me and land in the doctor's hands.

Words flooded my mind. Suddenly creation, survival, fittest, infinity, miracle, and God made more sense to me than ever before. God was manifesting itself through its sheer light of being. This was a God who was not divided by sects or any other barriers. I sensed a God of creation, love, and harmony.

The baby's one-month-premature body was held upside down in the air, its little feet in the doctor's hand. It was receiving its first punishment for being born, a friendly slap on the bottom. It started crying and was soon placed on my breast.

"It's a girl," said the nurse. I closed my eyes and hugged my baby as tightly as I could.

"She is Tara-Jane," I said.

Jaleh was offered the ritual of cutting the umbilical cord. She was horrified but did it. She later said she was so numb from having witnessed the birth she thought she might cut her own finger, too.

Because Tara-Jane was premature, she had to be kept in an incubator for five days. Jaleh gave Houshang the news, and the two of them joined me in my room. Houshang was exhausted from running around town, taking care of his work and anticipating the birth of his child, but he was thrilled to have a little girl.

Houshang and I looked at each other for a long time. Something had changed between us. He was not the same man. He looked far more mature.

My grandmother used to say, "If you want to know how someone feels about you, ask your heart the truth." My heart was telling me that Houshang and I were in love more than ever. We were one, cherishing the birth of the eternal bond between us.

"What is love?" Rumi was once asked. "You would not know until you become us," he replied.

A happy maternity-ward nurse came to let us know that they would be bringing Tara-Jane to me in a half hour, so I could breast-feed her. I asked Houshang to hand me my makeup bag. He asked why I needed it, and I said I wanted to look good for my first long encounter with my daughter, since they had taken her away so quickly the first time.

The nurses brought Tara-Jane in and left her with us. We were all over her, admiring her thick black hair and her big brown eyes as we caressed her doll-size feet. Houshang kindly suggested that she looked like me, but I could see how Houshang's strong genes had won the battle of chromosomes.

We left the hospital with Tara-Jane in my arms five days later. It was a perfect day, with the sun shining through the clouds. I felt like I was walking on the moon with my bundle of joy in my arms and my husband at my side.

31

A QUEST

Houshang's play was set to premiere in five days. We were still living with Farhad and waiting to move into our own apartment. We took Tara to Farhad's and put her on our king-size bed. She looked so small there. We looked at each other, wondering if she was going to be a petite girl. Little did we know she would be almost six feet one day. (She is now a head taller than me and calls me her "little mommy" every time she hugs me.)

Tara had to sleep between the two of us for the first few nights, until we moved to our own place. I would wake up at her littlest movements or cries, and always tended to her needs. Sometimes I would take her to the living room, bundled in her pink blanket, trying not to awaken Houshang and Farhad.

I would sit on the couch facing the window with my legs crossed—my favorite yoga position—and place Tara safely on my lap, holding on to her back with my left hand and helping her rest her soft and fragile little head on my chest as I directed her rosebud lips to my breast. Tara-Jane was content, and warm, sleeping like an angel when I would wake up at five o'clock in the morning, still sitting cross-legged.

I called my mother one morning and begged her to forgive me for ever hurting her when I was a child. My mother used to say that although mother and child live in two different bodies, they are created of one essence and soul. So when one is in pain, the other one feels the pain, too, no matter how far apart they are. I had no knowledge of what motherhood meant or felt like until I held Tara.

I told my mother how much I loved my daughter, and how afraid I was of making a mistake with her or losing her. I asked my mother how long this fear would last. She said, "Until you die."

HOUSHANG'S PLAY PREMIERED at the Lincoln Auditorium. I took Tara backstage and introduced her to the cast. Watching my colleagues onstage, I decided to ask Houshang if I could bring Tara out during the final scene, a demonstration against the Fundamentalist regime.

"I would like to bring her on in the final scene. I want to be like the thousands of Iranian mothers who bring their children to the demonstrations to echo the voice of the youth in Iran."

Houshang loved the idea, and Tara and I joined the crowd on the stage. The funny thing was that she slept peacefully in my arms throughout the whole scene. She was already a veteran actor.

WE FINALLY MOVED into our own place, a boxy two-bedroom apartment on the second floor of a typical 1960s cement residential building, painted in beige.

Houshang was desperate to take the play on tour across the United States, but the cost of touring with twenty players was too high. He began working on his next play instead and wanted me to stay home and take care of Tara. Despite his best effort to take care of everything, I began to worry. I was worried about the day we would not be able to pay the rent. I was worried about having to choose between either saving for Tara's education or paying our next utility bills. I had given birth to her in a free country so she could become who she wanted to be. I had saved her from a brutal religious tyranny in Iran. But I had exposed her to an insecure and uncertain future.

I started looking for a job when Tara was three months old. I first called the producer of an Iranian TV show, an international cable TV station, which broadcast shows in Farsi in California.

The producer had been in touch with me in the past about working on his hourlong show, which aired on Sundays. I went to see him, and he offered me a ten-minute segment on his show in Farsi. He was looking for an angle that would connect with the Iranian audience and wanted me to come up with a fresh new idea.

I had heard many true stories among Los Angeles's Iranian community that shared one common theme: nostalgia. I decided to write some nostalgic short essays about immigrants like myself and tell them to the audience. I would compare the past to the present, and then question the possibilities of tomorrow, in a sense echoing the voices of millions of people like me.

I named my segment "The City of Angels," and I began working on it right away. Once a week, Tara and I went in to record. She would watch me delivering my words to the camera, telling stories of my birth country.

Iranians who lived in the Los Angeles area loved the segment and kept encouraging me, sending supportive letters to the station.

TARA WAS ONE when the Iranian director Farrokh Majidi invited me to Denmark to portray an Iranian actress in exile in his movie *Raha*—which means "free."

I loved the story and could relate to the character wholeheartedly. I brought Tara with me, and the director's wife took care of her while we filmed. It took less than a month and was fairly successful with Iranian audiences in Europe and the United States.

Back in L.A., I kept working on the segment for the Iranian TV show and was also offered the hosting job at a Farsi-speaking morning radio show on the only Iranian radio station in L.A. It would be on weekdays from ten in the morning until noon.

I was still afraid to drive. Unwilling to burden Houshang further by asking him for rides to and from the station, I decided to travel by bus. My friends thought I was joking and laughed at me, but I wanted to do this. I had never hosted a radio show before, and I also wanted to prove to my friends that one could live in L.A. without having to drive.

I left home at eight-thirty every morning. Tara and I traveled an hour and a half by bus to the radio station. Our fellow passengers came from all backgrounds. An Iranian carpet seller, who traveled with a different small silk carpet rolled under his arm every morning, claimed it was safer to go to work on a bus. He was once held up at a gas station and robbed of a $10,000 silk carpet and his car, which unfortunately was not insured. His wife would give him a ride to Ventura Boulevard and wait with him until the bus arrived. In the afternoons I would see him carrying two large brown bags. One contained ripe oranges and the other Granny Smith apples.

I still remember the day he lost control of the bag of oranges. All the passengers were on their knees, trying to catch them. The poor bus driver told everyone to get back to their seats, but they were having fun, just like a bunch of kids.

When I arrived at the radio station, I would put Tara in her stroller with her favorite doll and stroke her hair while I was live on the air. Two hours of live radio required a lot of material and research. I would highlight the news in the first hour, and then have my listeners call in during the second half of the show. I asked them what their favorite topics were so everyone could share their opinions live on Radio-Sedaye-Iran (the voice of Iran on radio). Our conversations truly ran the gamut.

As much as I enjoyed my new profession, I felt bad dragging Tara to work every day. She needed to play and have fun. I was now working three jobs—radio host, TV host, and house-keeper. I was earning a decent amount of money at this point. Houshang was busy on another play. We decided to hire a nanny and found Christina, a wonderful woman whom Tara loved and who loved her back.

Tara-Jane was growing fast. Her curly brown hair surrounded her full cheeks and her large brown eyes. She was quiet and loved music. I would put her on the couch, surrounded by pillows and her dolls, turn on the stereo, and do my homework for my TV and radio shows well into the night.

The success of my program convinced a real estate agency to offer me the opportunity to host and produce a half-hour TV show on the same channel, sponsored by the agency. My friend and colleague Vatche Mangasarian, with whom I had had the pleasure of working in the movie *The Guests of Hotel Astoria*, would also be hosting a segment of the show and talk about the new movies of the week.

Vatche had been trying his best to convince me to get an agent, or to at least meet with his. He had worked in movies and TV for nearly two decades when I met him and thought I was wasting my time on the outskirts of Hollywood. He introduced me to his agent, David. He was very supportive and nice, and I loved his honesty. He told me that I was basically overqualified for the roles he was going to send me out to audition for.

A week later he sent me to audition for a guest role, the attaché's wife, on the soap opera *The Bold and the Beautiful*. Vatche was regularly portraying the attaché and had pitched me to be in it as his wife. I was more than happy to hear that I had gotten the part. I had one line: "Good evening, Your Majesty." The show aired in 1989.

Next my agent sent me on an audition for an Indian role. I told him I did not speak a word of Hindi, but he said it didn't matter. I went to the studio and noticed a couple of Indian women, almost my age, walking into the casting office before me. They looked beautiful in their traditional Indian dresses. I was in my jeans and a buttoned-down shirt. There was no way I could compete with them. I walked right out.

On the other hand, my third audition was simply odd. David sent me to an office on Hollywood Boulevard and said I had to be there by no later than four in the afternoon. He said it was for a movie called *Mission to Mars*. The scene I was auditioning for took place at a women's luncheon. But I was so preoccupied trying to find someone to give me a ride to the audition that I forgot I hadn't spoken with him about the role. I was at the door of a casting office when I noticed the sign on the door that read NUDITY REQUIRED.

I paused for a second and thought, first of all, David would have told me if this was the case. Secondly, what does *Mission to Mars* have to do with nudity?

"Are you looking for something?" asked a beautiful girl.

I told her what I was there for. She smiled and said that I was on the wrong floor. One floor up, a line of gorgeous, tall, white and blond actresses was waiting for their names to be called. I was sure I was in the wrong place yet again. The two young assistants looked at me in puzzlement and asked how they could help. When I said my agent had sent me, they handed me the designated parts of the script to read, and I prepared to audition.

I looked at the script in disbelief. The audition was for an astronaut's wife, and the scene was taking place at her home with a couple of other astronauts' wives, celebrating their husbands' mission to Mars. I left thinking I was *definitely* in the wrong place. I was neither tall enough, nor was I blond enough, and I was not exactly from Texas or anywhere else in the South. I wondered what David was thinking.

Another time, I went on a casting call for a small part and was sent home because I was "too beautiful" to play a down-trodden Middle Eastern woman.

I was finally able to break into Hollywood in 1990. I was cast as a saleslady in the episode "Nowhere to Turn," on *Matlock*, starring the late Andy Griffith. Andy Griffith was kind and invited me to have tea with him on our breaks. He often asked me questions about Iran. "Do you wish you could go back there?" is a question I hear all the time. In return, I always say that I will never go back to Iran until it is free. When the *Matlock* episode aired, Houshang threw a small party and tossed confetti into the air. Jaleh cracked a joke and said, "As the line in *All About Eve* goes, 'Fasten your seat belts, it's going to be a bumpy ride.'" (Yes, yes . . . I know the quote ends in "night," but Jaleh recalled it as "ride.")

32

DISSENT

VATCHE'S SUPPORT MEANT a lot to me, and I decided to take the real estate agency's offer and work with him on the show. I would give an introduction and Vatche would do a seven-minute segment, "Talk with Artists," in which he would either speak with well-known Iranian artists or review the top movie of the week in the United States, sometimes with expert guests.

It still makes me laugh every time I remember how Vatche and I pleasantly fought over the minutes in our show. It was twenty-eight minutes long, and we had to leave eight minutes out for the real estate agency's ads. But we kindly lent each other time when we knew a segment was too perfect to cut.

Garnik and Amalia Keshishian from the real state agency offered me a small office in the corner of their agency. Amalia was an incredibly kindhearted woman. She asked me if I would like to move into one of their properties in Tarzana in the Valley in return for half of the salary I had originally asked for.

I immediately accepted the offer. We were already paying a lot of money for a dinky apartment. We soon moved into a beautiful one-story, two-bedroom house, with a charming backyard and a white gazebo at the middle.

ONE EARLY MORNING while Houshang was in Paris visiting his sister, I received a worried call at home from Amalia. She said that my office had been ransacked and the outgoing message on the answering machine had been changed to a hate message from a jihadist. "I am a jihadist and I will put a bomb in your office. I will fucking kill you, you fucking infidels."

Garnik picked me up in ten minutes. They had already reported the incident to the police, and two gentlemen from the FBI soon joined them at the office. They were going over the scene when a call came in at eight-thirty in the morning. They asked me to pick up the phone and see if it was the jihadist. It was. They told me to try and engage him for as long as I could so they could trace his call.

The caller immediately bombarded me with obscenities. He called me names including "whore," "traitor," "infidel," and hung up before I had a chance to say anything in return. I was shocked. The authorities asked what I thought might have ignited such hate.

Suddenly I remembered the last time I was on Vatche's segment a few nights before. We had reviewed the movie *Not Without My Daughter*, starring Sally Field. The movie was based on a true story about an American woman, played by Sally Field, who was married to an Iranian, portrayed by the British actor Alfred Molina. The couple visits Iran, but when the wife discovers that her abusive husband intends to keep the family there permanently, she escapes the country with her daughter.

I was very vocal in defense of the wife and of women in similar situations in Iran. Vatche asked what if the story was not based on real events or actual facts. I said, "Come on, everyone knows some Iranian men beat their wives to death in the postrevolutionary Iran. They take advantage of Islamic law."

The third call came less than an hour later, and it was more of the same. I listened carefully this time to see if I could recognize his accent. It sounded Arabic, but his abusive language was similar to that used by prison interrogators in the Islamic Republic, using graphic sexual language to intimidate and bully. He kept calling me every hour, cursing and describing in detail how I was going to be raped by them if I did not shut my filthy mouth. Each call lasted less than a minute, so the police could not trace him.

Around two o'clock in the afternoon, he called again. I picked up the phone and lashed out at him. I was so sick and tired of his ugly and obscene words that I could not take it anymore. I cursed wildly and was stunned at how many words I could say in less than a minute. All he managed to say was that he would take care of me—he did not call back again.

The police asked me if I had any idea what stopped the caller. I said I thought I knew.

"He must be a Middle Easterner," I said. "He was caught off guard and offended at having let a woman use obscene words toward him. He wasn't used to it."

The police and FBI did their best to look after us for a while, but the man never called back again.

If Houshang had been home, he would have been devastated and furious. I told him about the incident later, and he unsurprisingly became angry. He wanted me to stop working on the show. I reminded him that I was practicing the First Amendment, and that I was not going to sit back and be harassed by a thug.

33

THE SWEET SCENT OF LOVE

MEANWHILE I WAS putting all my energy and love into Tara, who was now almost three. She had a strong personality and was beautiful. Her pink-white skin, curly brown hair, big almond-shaped brown eyes, and pinchable cheeks stopped everyone in their tracks. We were even approached by a director of commercials who said Tara would be perfect for baby beauty pageants or a baby commercial. I thanked the gentleman but let him know we were not interested in his offer. Houshang and I had both started acting on our own initiative. Nobody had made us do it. We did not want to force Tara into a world that may or may not be the one she would want to live in.

Houshang had finished writing his new play, *The Sweet Scent of Love*. It revolved around a childless couple in their midthirties. The two are on the verge of a nasty breakup, bombarding each other with abusive words, but a sudden visit from the woman's uncle forces them to put their dispute on hold. The uncle's wisdom, plus his gifts from Iran, bring back the loving memories of their early days in their birth country. This sense of nostalgia sparks a reconciliation between the two. Houshang and I were lucky enough to have Daryoush Irani-Nejad, a prominent Iranian actor, portray the uncle while we played the bickering couple.

The three of us read and rehearsed the play in the evenings in our small living room so we could keep an eye on Tara. She would play with her dolls and watch us. I am sure she was wondering what her parents were up to, kissing each other one minute and getting mad at each other the next. She would get worried every time we shouted at each other. But we would make faces to distract her and get her to laugh.

Whenever Houshang wrote a new play, we usually rented a large performance venue for a couple of nights in L.A. like many other theatrical groups. But the time had come for us to rent a permanent place to perform. We decided to form a theater company whose meaningful and humorous plays would make it the most successful Farsi-speaking theater company outside of Iran. We named our company Work Shop '79, after the workshop in Iran and the year that changed all of our lives. Our workshop is still running today and recently celebrated its twentieth anniversary.

We were also lucky to find an affordable place in the heart of the San Fernando Valley, in the "Valley of Iranians," in the city of Encino. The Comedy Club of Encino was a small venue with a capacity of 180 seats. It was busy during the week, so the owner could only let us rent it on Sundays. Considering the importance of the location and its short distance from our home, we decided to take the club owner's offer and rent the place for a year, having two performances on Sundays with an option to renew the contract annually.

AFTER A MONTH and a half of rehearsals, and a restoration of the club, we performed the play and were thrilled to find that the audience not only connected with the story but also found it incredibly funny.

We ran our business with family and friends. My youngest brother, Shahrokh—now Sean—an engineer and computer tech, helped us with the light and sound. My sister-in-law Soraya, who was married to Houshang's brother, took care of the box office. Farhad managed the stage.

Our shows on Sundays were sold out weeks in advance. I looked at the reservation sheets and noticed that a couple of the same names kept appearing week after week. I asked one of them if she had seen the play before, and she said she had seen it sixteen times, bringing her friends and family and, more important, guests from Iran. She said she enjoyed it more and more every time she watched it.

Parents brought their older kids to get a sense of Iranian humor when it comes to love and divorce. Iranian psychologists and family consultants sent their clients to see the play. Young couples contemplating divorce came to see the realistic portrayal of a marriage in disarray and then repair, and were happy in the end. No matter how idealistic the solution may have seemed, the play worked well with its audience.

Little did we know that the play, *The Sweet Scent of Love*, was going to have a place on the stage for four consecutive years. Thousands of Iranians came to see it in more than six hundred performances, both in L.A. and on tours throughout the U.S.A., Canada, Australia, and Europe. Houshang had his first hit, and I made my real debut on the Iranian-American stage.

I was also up to my second role in a TV series. In 1993, I played Malika, the wife of a shopkeeper, on *Martin*, starring Martin Lawrence. I was amazed that before the taping Martin asked the cast to join hands and pray for a good show. It showed a sense of camaraderie that reminded me of Iran.

34

SAFETY BELT

WE MANAGED TO buy our first house in Woodland Hills, in the Valley right outside of L.A. It was a conventional but beautiful three-bedroom, one-story house, located on a hill in a neighborhood of similar houses built in the 1960s. To me it shouted the American Dream. It was close to three thousand square feet, with a backyard that was almost half an acre. A small swimming pool was located next to an olive tree in the middle of the yard. We built a platform in the back and created an outdoor stage. Though we never actually performed there, we would use it to host two contemporary Iranian painters and their small exhibitions. By the early 1990s, Houshang and I wanted to share our financial success with our fellow Iranian artists by supporting and collecting their works.

Charles Hossein Zenderoudi, an accomplished and sophisticated master of combining calligraphy with the art of painting residing in France, had a unique vision and a spiritual mind.

His exquisite calligraphies and abstract studies were colorful and reminiscent of the French masters of the nineteenth century. Zenderoudi was coming to visit his family in the U.S.A., and we asked him if we could throw a private exhibition for him at our house.

Our second guest artist was Reza Yah Yaei, an incredible sculptor and painter who lives in a village on the border of France and Italy. We asked him to exhibit his works at our house as well, and he loved the idea.

By this time, my ex-husband, Aydin, had become a famous painter whose work was collected by Europeans and Americans, selling for tens of thousands of dollars, and auctioned by Bonham's, Sotheby's, and Christie's. His portrait of me is still in my living room. Today we remain in touch sporadically by phone. Pasha and Aydin's mother had passed away of old age, and he and his second wife now had a daughter, too. Our daughters are only a year apart, yet they have never met. They are both named Tara.

With the success of our play, I received an offer from another Iranian television show, *Jam-E-Jam*, which aired on Sunday afternoons. *Jam-E-Jam* hosted a number of great political debates and interviews with well-known American, Israeli, and former Iranian politicians, as well as countless political analysts and talking heads. It was a great platform for me to discuss more serious matters.

In truth, Amalia and her real estate agency could not afford to support their show any longer. One of us had to put an end to it, so I did. I went to her and asked for her blessing to leave. She was both sad and relieved.

WITH OUR MOVE to Woodland Hills, Tara was now going to a French-speaking kindergarten and I was working constantly. (Speaking French was a sign of nobility back in Iran. It was a cultural tradition we intended to keep.) The school was called LILA, and if nothing else, knowing a few languages—including Farsi and Spanish from her nanny—could always get Tara a job at the United Nations.

I had to start driving again, but I was frightened. A friend suggested that I get a driving instructor who was familiar with psychology. Believe it or not, I found one who fit the bill. Mr. Ali was a driving instructor who specialized in helping people traumatized by past car accidents.

Mr. Ali picked me up at home and asked me to drive around the neighborhood. I sat nervously behind the wheel and started driving slowly. He asked me to go a little faster, and then began telling me about his first wife, who had divorced him and married an American military officer. We did a couple of loops around the neighborhood and went home.

During our second session Mr. Ali told me about his second wife. After his divorce, he visited Iran and married an Iranian girl and brought her to the United States. But she, too, divorced him after she received her green card. I was getting antsy circling the same streets and waiting at red lights while Mr. Ali told me about his second divorce and depression. I headed toward the entry ramp for highway 101 heading south. Suddenly he looked at me and said, "Oh, now you drive on highways!"

Shortly after Mr. Ali started telling me about his third wife, I passed the DMV's written exam and driving test. I have no idea if he had a fourth wife. I was just happy to be driving again.

I named my first car in America—a secondhand—after my beloved Sanjar.

JAM-E-JAM COULD NOT meet my salary request but offered to supplement the difference with two great spots for Houshang and me to advertise our plays. I had left Iran to get an audience and to do what I could to shed light on the injustices going on in my birth country. This would be a great platform for me to make my contribution to the people of Iran. I could put my degree in international relations to good use, and I gladly accepted *Jam-E-Jam*'s offer.

AYATOLLAH KHOMEINI PASSED away in 1989, and Ayatollah Ali Khamenei, who had been the president of Iran since 1981, was now the supreme leader of Iran. Much like their similar names, Khamenei's regime was virtually indistinguishable from Khomeini's.

The Islamic Republic was at its peak in 1992, maintaining religious fascism with the help of its notorious intelligence service, SAVAMA. People disappeared in broad daylight, and their families were considered lucky if they were told where they could find the bodies of their loved ones. Hundreds of young Iranians, men and women alike, were being captured, raped, tortured, and sentenced to death for religious or political beliefs different from those dictated by the regime.

JAM-E-JAM ASKED ME to open the show with a five-to-seven-minute monologue. I was free to choose the topic of the week.

Mr. Bebian, the executive producer, was a man of substance. He was Jewish and although he had to leave Iran with his family out of fear of being persecuted, he still loved Iran, even though he had not been fortunate enough to pursue a higher education there. His biggest wish was to see the country free, and he did his best to enlighten and educate Iranian viewers through *Jam-E-Jam*'s sociopolitical and entertaining Sunday shows.

Bebian said that although he was not going to censor me or ask me to cover a certain topic if I did not want to, there was one thing he wanted me to remember when writing my monologues: "Even though our show is a local one, and only gets aired in L.A., its copies travel far away. In fact, it will go as far as remote villages in Iran. It will be taken there on the back of donkeys carrying rice, beans, onions, and other illegal tapes of Farsi-speaking shows produced outside Iran. Just remember what a vast and versatile audience you have."

Iranian TV shows produced in L.A. were hot on the black market. After all, Iranian-American films and shows were powerful evidence of successful Iranians living in a democratic society.

There was no official relationship between the two countries at the time, nor is there today. Ayatollah Khomeini had once made it clear that the Islamic Republic of Iran is a package that does not include the U.S.A. And it seemed like America had washed her hands of Iran after the hostage crisis, where fifty-two Americans were held captive for 444 days, from November 4, 1979, to January 20, 1981.

MY FIRST TALK on *Jam-E-Jam* covered Fereydoun Farokhzad, who was an Iranian actor, singer, poet, TV and radio host, and an opposition political figure.

He had been involved in producing an opposition radio program and was chased by Islamic Republic assassins in Germany prior to his tragic death. Allegedly he had been advised to stop criticizing the regime on his popular, politically driven radio show. He was told that he could return to Iran if he stopped performing his shows. He could see his mother, whom he loved, and also receive a handsome amount of money. Fereydoun was subsequently slaughtered in his apartment in Bonn, at the age of fifty-three. Three men were rumored to have been tracking him. He was stabbed all over his body, and his throat was slashed. The assassins were never found.

My viewers were overwhelmed by my first segment. I went on to write *Jam-E-Jam*'s Sunday opening talks for twelve years. I spoke about the torture chambers in Evin, and the rape of political prisoners (regardless of their age) as much as I talked about road rage, gang rape, pedophiles, and identity theft in the U.S.A.

I would again be harassed by thugs, who sent faxes to *Jam-E-Jam*, calling me names and threatening me. I found the copy shop from which the faxes had been sent and learned that they had a surveillance camera. The shop owner said he needed police permission to show me the video. I was so angry I went to the police station in Burbank and filed a complaint.

I was dead tired when I got back to *Jam-E-Jam* that afternoon. Bebian was bewildered at what I had done. He had called in his lawyer to talk to me.

The lawyer asked, "Why do you bother getting involved with these thugs and cowards? They're all bark and no bite. Suppose you find them and put them on trial? Do you really want your name and your picture next to these bastards? On the front page?

"It is good that you have filed a complaint, but I would not pursue it if I were you unless we receive another threat. Do you still want to follow up with the case or drop it?"

I chose to drop it and move on.

35

RED LIGHT, GREEN LIGHT

OUR NEXT PLAY, *Our Father's Heritage*, written and directed by Houshang, was more on the somber side and ran successfully for two years in Los Angeles and toured throughout the U.S.A., Europe, Australia, and Canada. But it was easily the most troublesome we put onstage.

Our play premiered to a sold-out crowd in Vancouver at Centennial Hall, a well-known professional theater with a nice-size stage, a great Canadian crew, and a capacity of six hundred seats. The show started on time at eight o'clock, and I wasn't due onstage until about fifteen minutes into the performance. I was sitting in the dressing room, facing the mirror, when a German shepherd that looked very much like Pasha came into the room. I turned around and saw he was followed by a couple of Canadian policemen. I was speechless.

The police had received a bomb threat and had to stop the

play and evacuate the theater. I asked them to let me relay the news to the audience, and they kindly let me. I'll never forget the look on Houshang's face that night. He can be quite particular about stage directions, sometimes to the point of obsession. I was onstage five minutes early.

I smiled at Houshang and the other actors, walked to the center of the stage, and calmly told the audience we had received a bomb threat and needed everyone to leave the building as quickly as possible.

I still feel like crying every time I remember how gracefully our Iranian audience left the theater, knowing their lives were in danger. They did not run, did not push and shove each other. They did not even try to get ahead of one another. They just walked out and waited for two hours in the adjacent parking lot for the police to thoroughly search the building.

Unfortunately the theater had to close before midnight and we could not resume the play after the police were done with their work. We asked the audience to turn in their tickets and get their money back, but nobody wanted to. They said they would hold on to them for another night. Sadly, we were heading to Toronto the following day, but our sponsor promised that he would book another date and bring us back soon.

He also told us that the number of fanatical Iranian Muslims in Canada was growing at an alarming rate. People who held key positions in the Islamic Republic of Iran had chosen Canada as a home away from home, running successful businesses in Iran out of Canada.

A Farsi-speaking weekly show in Canada interviewed us afterward, and I did not shy away from letting its Iranian audience know how disturbing the whole incident was to all of us. I also mentioned that we would be back to perform the play. "I for one am not threatened by some leeches fed by the Fundamentalists!" I said.

Two months later, we were back in Vancouver. This time the theater was ready for any disturbance. The police had installed two metal detectors at the entrance. A dozen policemen and a couple of trained dogs searched the place thoroughly before the audience came in.

All the ticket holders were back, and our sponsor had to turn away newcomers. Six hundred people sat in the theater to watch what they had missed two months before. It was amazing to me that they, too, did not care about the bogus bomb threat, even though the Canadian police had taken it very seriously.

The show started at eight o'clock sharp with a couple of policemen waiting backstage. I was talking with the chief of police when an officer came in and told us they had received another bomb threat. I said, "But your men have searched the room. We know it's phony."

I was told that according to the law they had to evacuate the place. I delivered the bad news, and the audience again gathered in the parking lot. We managed to talk to as many people as we could. They were all very supportive of us and, again, said they would hold on to their tickets until they could see the play.

On our third attempt, we managed to stage our play in Vancouver. I was told months later that there were rumors that one of the actors had disabled the main switchboard at the theater before showtime.

HOUSHANG WAS DYING to write a musical, a modern version of
an Iranian fable called *Amir-Arsalan*, the story of a princess im-
prisoned by a beast. I was not very keen on the idea. I felt that
the message and the content of the play were too outdated for
our Iranian audience. It was 1998, and most of them had lived
outside Iran for nearly twenty years. And there was the fact that
Iranians had not shown a lot of interest in musicals before.
Houshang could not be swayed.

What followed was two months of rehearsals that included
dance and voice training. A sum of $125,000 dollars from our
own pockets was invested in creating an original score, sophisticated portable sound system, props and costumes designed by
my friend Pari Malek, the designer of my borrowed wedding
gown.

Unfortunately I was right. The musical was not as successful
as our past plays. To say the least, it created tension in our
house. And I realized I needed a vacation.

TARA AND I took a trip to Yellowstone National Park on a tour
with other mostly Iranian mothers and their daughters. I was
extremely happy, having Tara next to me at all times, on such a
heavenly journey through the grandeur of the Wild West and
its spectacular features.

As much as I enjoyed having quality time with Tara, I was
sad to learn how little these Iranian daughters knew about their
mothers' pasts. It was during this trip to Yellowstone when I
decided to write my own one-woman show, based on the many
stories I had either heard or experienced during my life's journey. I called it *The Other Half.*

Best described, it was seven episodes in a woman's life, connected to one another by contemporary popular songs such as "Strangers in the Night," sung by Frank Sinatra, that played over and over again in the late 1960s at the Palace of Ice on Pahlavi Boulevard.

In the first episode the woman is six years old and listening to her grandmother's bedtime story. Then she goes through her teens, thriving, growing into a young woman, getting married and having to flee her birth country. Finally she successfully immigrates to England. In the last episode, she is chasing the sun in Hyde Park Corner in London. As she looks back on her life, she keeps talking and moving her chair toward sunspots.

The play was staged at the Comedy Club in Farsi for a couple of weeks for a limited engagement. It was directed by Houshang, who was pretty much the only male in attendance. Hundreds of Iranian mothers brought their daughters to see the play.

I cannot remember how many times I was approached by these daughters, who told me that, after seeing the play, they had a totally new perception of their mothers. One of them actually thanked me for showing her who her mother was. She told me she was born here in the United States and had no idea what sort of life her mother had led in the past.

I performed the play in Stockholm, Sweden, on March 8, 1999, on Woman's Day, to an audience of hundreds of Iranians. I performed it in Goteborg the following night. Again it was well received. I felt humbled by the audience's jubilant applause. I marveled that I was able to write a story, or rather convey my *own* story, in a way that allowed daughters to connect with their mothers. Tara came to see it a few times, once bringing me red roses at the end of the performance.

36

ALWAYS WITH MY DAUGHTER

TARA WAS ALREADY seven years old, still studying at LILA in Woodland Hills. It is fascinating how children grow in the blink of an eye. I was anxious for my parents to see Tara. They had to travel to Istanbul to apply for a visa at the American Embassy, since the U.S.A. no longer had one in Iran.

Tara and I took my parents to Disneyland, and they loved it, especially riding in the small teacups as the song "It's a Small World (After All)" played along and the colorful pastel teacups swirled about. I wish I could have had them longer, not only for my own sake but also for Tara's. They only stayed for two months and went home so soon that it still seems like it never happened. My father was incredibly polite and said that he did not want to be a burden on us. I tried to tell him that they would never be a burden on us, but he said I was married and had to think of my husband's privacy, too.

Tara was already a young girl with a lot of ambition. She wanted to become an astrologer, then an archaeologist. The list went on. She had her own close circle of friends, all from school, and they would speak French in her bedroom—I think because they knew I didn't understand it that well, and they wanted to talk about boys.

Tara also had a particular taste in clothing. She preferred casual clothes and flat shoes. I'll never forget the day I wanted to get her a designer top and she said she did not understand why she had to wear the designer's name on her shirt, having already paid for it.

Around this time I asked Tara if she wanted to learn to play an instrument, something my mother had wished for me but had never happened. She accepted the offer of piano lessons only if I stayed in the room while Madam Kazjanian taught her to play. I agreed, as I did years later when she needed extra help with math and algebra. I had sat at the back of the evening class with the permission of the school and her teacher while Tara was studying her math. The school may have thought that I was too protective of her, but this was my way of teaching Tara that I would do anything for her to get a better education, even if I had to sit in the classroom for two hours, realizing that my own math wasn't that good.

Although things weren't picture perfect with us, life seemed calm and promising. But far away, another disaster was about to consume my family.

37

EVIN

As a doctor in Tehran, my middle brother, Shahriar, had gone to a school sponsored by the military. He had risen through the ranks of the military regime to become the head of the Health Department for a division of the air force. As time passed, my brother was being pressured by the military to fulfill its ever increasing requirements, which included daily prayers. He did not approve of what was being imposed upon him and felt like he no longer belonged in Tehran's medical world. He fled Iran, having told authorities he was going on a short visit to London, though he never planned to return. His wife and children were supposed to join him later. But after about a year away, his wife urged his return to Iran with assurances that he would not face ramifications for fleeing Iran and the army.

His capture in Iran just so happened to be the day after a huge demonstration was held at the Federal Building in L.A., where ten thousand Iranians showed up. CNN had called me in advance and told me that they needed to tie a story to the demonstration. Houshang and I agreed to be interviewed.

I had met an Iranian student who had fled Iran after a year in Evin Prison. He had been beaten and tortured. One of his legs was an inch shorter than the other after being pulled in a torture session. In graphic detail on CNN, I spoke about him and the torture chambers he had been through.

The next day my brother was put in Evin Prison, accused of having passed military information to the British. He was charged with being a spy. He was interrogated and asked if he had anything to do with what I had said on CNN about torture chambers in Iran.

The conditions at Evin are horrid. Shahriar was interrogated and beaten and held for a year. Because of his skills as a doctor, though, the other prisoners and officials sought him out with their medical complaints, and he helped them as best he could. He wasn't allowed any visitors, which was very hard on my family. My parents were the ones who suffered the most, dreading the possible execution of their son. Upon his release he was officially dismissed from the army and stripped of his medical degree.

When he eventually left Iran again, this time for good, he went to Istanbul. He couldn't practice medicine since his medical license and degrees had been taken away by the army in Iran, but my parents helped him as he tried to figure out what he was going to do next. Unfortunately he had to leave his family behind, including his three children. He would eventually divorce his wife for her own safety.

38

THAT DAY

HOUSHANG HAD FINISHED writing his newest play, *Happiness Plus Tax*, and we were getting ready for rehearsals when Shahla called and told me she was going to leave the States and live in a village in India called Rishe-Kash. She had divorced her husband and visited India with a friend of hers earlier that year. She was taken by the poor children of the village and had decided to sell her properties in Northern California and start a free school for them.

I was so happy for her. Being friends since our youth, I knew this was what she wanted and would make her happy in life. Tara and I traveled to San Francisco to say good-bye to her. We went to bed early that night, since she no longer had a TV or a radio.

It was seven-thirty in the morning when Shahla's father called us and told us that the Twin Towers had been hit by terrorists. We were stunned. I was horrified at the tragedy and could not believe Shahla did not have a television.

We went to her neighbor's house across the street and asked if we could watch the news with him. We watched in horror. We saw the people of New York running, shouting, and crying. Bewildered, they searched for their loved ones who worked in the area. I'll never forget the image of mothers screaming and racing to their children's schools.

I wept and felt deeply sad and sorry to have witnessed the massacre of thousands of innocent people by Muslim terrorists and the effect it might have on our children.

Our host did not let us leave until long after lunch. I was overwhelmed by his graciousness. After all, his country had been attacked by people who looked like us and were of the same religion. But he wanted us to know that he was aware of the difference and that we were always welcome at his house. Perhaps his attitude is a general one in the U.S.A. I have never been discriminated against after 9/11 for being a Middle Easterner. Still, perhaps I am just one of the lucky ones, as I know others have faced unfair searches and other injustices because of their names and the traditional Muslim garments that they wear.

Shahla left a few days later to start her Mother Miracle School in India. Today it has more than five hundred students, whose families are also cared for with the help of Shahla's family and friends who sponsor the kids. Houshang and I are sponsoring seven of them.

A VACATION WITH Tara was long overdue. We needed some quality time together, so the two of us took a trip to London to spend New Year's with my brother Shahram and his family.

Tara asked me if we could go to Westminster Abbey's Midnight Mass. I always wanted to go to one when I lived in

London but never had the opportunity. My friend Pari came along with us.

Westminster Abbey's Gothic architecture, magnificent statues, stained-glass work, and grand paintings looked even more heavenly when the church choir began singing "Ave Maria" and the spirit of Christmas took over the ceremony. We left after one o'clock in the morning, having had a divine experience. We soon discovered there was no transportation available. Pari and I had lived in London long enough to know that there is no public transportation running at that hour and that we should have reserved a car to pick us up. We had no choice but to walk all the way home. Snow covered the ground, and the trees and Christmas lights were now turned off, except for the ones shining off of Buckingham Palace and the Houses of Parliament.

We walked down Victoria Street at Parliament Square, and kept going till we reached the queen's palace. There was not a soul in the square when the three of us got there. We danced and whirled in the snow on ice in front of the palace and waved our hands to say hello to the queen.

We crossed through St. James Park to take a shortcut to our apartment. The park was dark, cold, and eerie. Five minutes into our walk, I knew I had made a mistake and should have taken us through the streets, but I did not say a word. Instead I tried to be funny and kept singing and encouraged them to sing along with me. Pari was dead tired and was quiet. Tara said the park reminded her of the movie *Sleepy Hollow*. She then reminded me of what I had told her had happened in the same park when I was residing in London—a man had killed a couple of people with an ax in the middle of the night.

The three of us started running. We reached Piccadilly Street and soon were close to our place. We were starving and bought a couple of sandwiches from a store that was open all night. Just seeing the cashier made me feel safe.

It was now almost four o'clock in the morning. I wanted Tara to see where I lived in London when I was a bachelorette and took a detour past number 40 on the corner of Warwick Avenue facing the canal. There was not a soul on the street when we got there.

Tara was so excited, but Pari was begging us to go home. We were about to cross the street when two thuggish-looking young guys appeared out of nowhere. One of them stopped us, and the other one stood behind us, next to the Warwick Underground station. The station was deep below the street, and they could have dragged us there if they attacked us.

Tara was standing next to me, frightened. I held her hand, with the plastic bag packed with sandwiches hanging from my right arm, and took a good hold of my umbrella with my left hand. I looked straight into the guy's eyes and held his gaze. He was not more than sixteen or seventeen years old, but was well built.

He said he wanted sex. Calmly letting go of Tara's hand, and not taking my eyes off of his, I showed him the plastic bag and asked him if he would like a sandwich. He laughed sadistically and shouted to the other boy.

"Did you hear sandwiches?" He laughed. He looked at me and said it again. "I need sex."

I took a deep breath and asked, "Do I look like someone who is interested in sex, young man?" And he laughed again.

His hand was reaching for his pocket when I shouted at the

other one who was keeping an eye on the street. I said, "For God's sake, ask him to stop it. Have some dignity."

To my relief he ordered the menacing guy to step off. We started walking away slowly and then faster. I could hear Pari's teeth clattering and told her she should not act like a mouse when in the presence of cats. We were home within a few minutes.

I had averted a disaster by staying composed, but it was a shame that such a peaceful residential area that I used to live in not long ago had changed so drastically. I felt sad for what once was. And to think it was Christmas!

39

SAND AND FOG

AT THE AGE of fourteen, Tara was looking more and more like a young woman. She was a teenager now. I was beginning to understand why my father was so worried when I was Tara's age. She was an only child. Although she had many friends, I really felt guilty for not giving her a brother or a sister. Houshang and I had made the decision to have only one child in order to give her the best education and life possible. Still, it hurt me to see her sitting alone in her room surfing the Internet.

Tara was in ninth grade at LILA when she told me she wanted to go to an American school.

"Mom, I am an American. I need to go to an American school and learn the system." She was right. As much as I loved LILA, I had to look for a new school, somewhere safe, with a good reputation, caring teachers, and large, clean, sunny classrooms.

I fell in love with Calabasas High School after a thorough search and was told that we had to live in the area for Tara to be able to attend the school. Houshang and I both knew that Tara's education was far more important than the house we both loved.

We did not have much time before school started. I was watching TV on a Sunday, wondering how on earth we were were going to find a place in less than a month. Flipping through the channels I found a real estate channel, and there it was. I could not believe my eyes. The house for sale on TV was in Calabasas and looked exactly like what we wanted. I called our agent, and later that day we went to see the house with the rain pouring down on us. The owner was not happy to be disturbed. I took only a quick peek before telling our agent on the spot that we would buy it. It was a spacious Spanish-style four-bedroom home, with four bathrooms, a pool, and Jacuzzi out back overlooking a golf course and the mountains of the Valley. It had a huge kitchen where I would cook traditional Persian meals. The house felt immediately like home.

Tara moved in and started her freshman year at Calabasas High.

HOUSHANG HAD WRITTEN a new play, *Our Sweet Life by the Pacific Ocean*, and wanted us to start rehearsals. I was happy to get back to work. A portrait of an Iranian family with a goth son and his girlfriend, the play was staged in 2002 and ran through 2003.

We were on our way to perform the play at the Palace of Fine Arts in San Francisco when our caravan stopped for refreshments at a roadside café. I got out of the car, hypnotized by a book Jaleh had given me. Oprah Winfrey had recommended *House of Sand and Fog*, by Andre Dubus III, for her book club back in 2000. She told her audience that, because it was so good, they ought to buy two copies and give one to a friend, which is how I received mine.

At the café I shared with Houshang what seemed like an impossible dream. I told him that I would be perfect to portray Nadi, the wife of Colonel Behrani, if the novel I was reading were turned into a film. "If Hollywood decides to make a film out of this book one day, it would be unfair of them not to give me the role. It will prove there is no democracy in this country," I added.

Houshang laughed and said, "You are such a political animal. What has this have to do with democracy? Who are *they*?"

Time went by, and I was chatting with Jaleh in my home office on a lazy afternoon in the heat of the Indian summer. I had recently come back from Europe and was telling her about the success of the tour and the unusual heat in Paris. The phone rang and I picked it up.

"May I talk to Soryia Abidaslooea?" the caller said.

"Wow, that sounds like my name, but it is not my name," I said.

The caller replied in a gentler voice, "Whatever your name is, would you like to come down and sort it out?"

"Come down to where?" I asked. "And what must I sort out?"

"Come to our casting office."

"Regarding . . . ?"

"Regarding the film that DreamWorks is about to shoot in L.A. *House of Sand and Fog*."

A sudden rush of blood in my heart brought back the memory of the panic attacks I had suffered when I began living in Los Angeles. All I could manage to say was, "When?"

The caller said, "As soon as possible," and asked me to audition at 10:00 A.M. on the following day. I must have looked really bad when I hung up the phone.

"What happened to you? Are you OK? You look like you have seen a ghost. Who was it?" Jaleh asked.

I told her who it was and then we both fell dead silent.

I did not have much time to prepare for the audition. One thing I was sure about was Nadi's rich and elegant look, the way I had imagined her when I read the book. I decided that perhaps her classic style compensated for all the sadness in her eyes.

While preparing dinner, I started working on the four scenes I would need to perform in the audition. Although I had been advised by so-called acting experts not to memorize the lines, I did what I always had. I made the lines my own by studying each and every word, and even throwing away words.

The character of Nadi was from a fairly reserved, well-off family. She was married to Colonel Behrani and had left Iran at the time of the revolution. On paper she and I were supposed to have a lot in common. But in reality we were two entirely different people. Unlike me, Nadi was quiet and shy. She was raised to get married, obey her husband, and give birth to as many beautiful, intelligent, and healthy children—preferably boys—as possible.

The writer Andre Dubus III had written enough of her background in the book for me to imagine the rest of her story, her childhood and teen years, for example. I wrote a one-page biography, as I always do when portraying a character. Then I started cutting out pictures from fashion magazines that would best represent her taste in clothing and her seemingly lavish lifestyle and placed them all in a scrapbook.

I woke up early the next day and reviewed the scenes several times until Jaleh came by to pick me up. She had said that she would take me there, so I could go through the lines with her in the car and not have to drive.

We arrived at the casting director's office. Debora Aquila taped my audition and said she would call me. She phoned the next day and asked me to audition for the director of the film, Vadim Perelman.

My first reaction to the second call was to think of a dress or a suit that Nadi would wear for a simple lunch. Jaleh and I went to Nordstrom's and purchased a straight saffron-colored skirt, complemented by lighter-color stitches on the sides. I also picked up a beige silk ruffled chemise and a pair of three-inch beige pumps.

Again I woke up early and went through the lines while putting on my makeup. I usually do not wear makeup during the day except for lipstick, but I was sure that Nadi would not leave the house unless she was perfectly coiffed.

Jaleh and I got to DreamWorks's studio at 11:00 A.M. We went through what seemed like endless, winding corridors, and finally found the room. I knocked on the door and opened it. All I saw was Debora telling me, "Oh no, you've got to wait for me."

I immediately closed the door. She came out within a few minutes and took me inside. I was then formally introduced to Vadim Perelman, the Russian-American director. This would be his first English-speaking feature film. After going through a couple of complimentary words, Vadim said, "I am planning to shoot this film with no makeup on. Do you mind coming back tomorrow not wearing any?"

He said he knew why I had dressed up as exquisitely as I imagined my character Nadi would. But he had to see me in much simpler attire. When I turned around to leave, I heard him say, "And see if you can make me cry!"

What I had learned from our encounter was invaluable. Never try to look like your character, leave some room for the director's imagination. Turn yourself into a blank canvas ready to be painted on. Give him the pleasure of discovering you rather than finding you.

The following morning I washed my face, put on jeans, and gathered my hair in a loose ponytail. I had no intention of using my shiny black hair as a dramatic tool to make the director cry.

Jaleh and I went back to the studio. The people in the room included Michael London, one of the producers of the film; the director, Vadim; and Debora and her cameraman. They were sitting around an oblong Formica table with Debora facing me and the cameraman next to her, taping my audition. Debora asked me if I needed to take pauses between scenes, and I said that I would rather not. Taking a pause would have distracted me. I needed to stay in character.

Debora started reading the lines with me, and I went into a trance, using all my power to forget where I was and who was there. I was imagining Nadi in a house with her family, responding to her husband's demands while trying to teach her son how to be a gentleman. I was sitting next to a wall and used it as an imaginary door.

In scene one, Nadi is in the kitchen, brewing tea, trying to teach her son how to be kind to the woman (Kathy) who has crashed on her son's bed in their house, which was once hers.

In scene two, Nadi is waiting for Kathy to join them for dinner, but Kathy does not leave the bathroom. Nadi knocks on the door a few times and then opens it to find that the woman has attempted suicide. Nadi saves the woman.

In scene three, Nadi blames her husband, Colonel Behrani, for the incident.

In the final scene of the audition, Nadi finds out that her son is dead. Staring at her husband's bloody shirt, she cries silently.

Pretending Debora was Colonel Behrani was easy, since she was whispering the colonel's lines and I kept staring at her shirt, imagining a trace of blood on it, as was mentioned in the script.

I was not forcing myself to cry. I was just trying to stay in that tragic moment when Nadi becomes aware of her son's death and, without admitting the truth through words, starts crying silently, still in a state of denial. It worked. I ended up crying silently, not daring to look up. Then I heard applause. It was Vadim. I looked over at him and gave him a devilish half smile and a wink, which he ended up including in the DVD extras for the film.

Vadim walked toward me. He bent down and kissed my forehead, whispering, "Welcome aboard."

I cried hard when I left the room. Poor Jaleh thought something must have gone wrong.

"What happened? Did you get it?" she asked.

"Yes, I got the role," I replied.

"Why are you crying then?" she said.

"Because my life is going to change," I answered.

I was now on my way to Hollywood for real.

I EVENTUALLY DISCOVERED that Ben Kingsley, my idol whom I had seen perform in London, would play my husband, and that the lovely and talented Jennifer Connelly would play Kathy. Jonathan Ahdout, a handsome young man of fifteen, would play my son.

We shot the film in Malibu, except for the fog scene, which was shot in San Francisco. Every morning at five, I would be driven to the set, either to the DreamWorks studio lot or to a home on the hills, overlooking the ocean.

We each had our own trailer, but Jennifer and I became friends and often spent our downtime together, either chatting or playing games. Our favorite was a game called "Off the Cliff." We would give each other three random names of popular Hollywood actors, and we had to choose which one we would enjoy sharing our bed with, which we would marry, and finally which we would send off the cliff.

Later on Ben Kingsley and I would play charades as we traveled through the United States to promote the film. On set, he was very much a method actor, staying in character.

The film came out in December 2003 to much acclaim. Oprah even did a segment on her talk show about the movie. I was unable to make it, as I was working in Baltimore on a pilot, but I would have loved to meet Oprah, to whom I owe my success for introducing me to such a powerful book.

I WAS FIRST nominated for an Independent Spirit award for my supporting role in *House of Sand and Fog*, followed by the Critics'

Choice award and the Los Angeles Film Critics Association award.

I was ecstatic when I heard the news of being nominated for an Independent Spirit award, and was shocked when my name was called out at the ceremony. One of my favorite actors, Forest Whitaker, announced my name—and did a perfect job in pronouncing it.

I could not believe my ears and was fixated on Vadim, my director. He smiled, and I looked at Houshang, then I heard Sir Ben saying, "It is you, my dear. What are you waiting for?" And I raced to the stage to receive my award, a bronze eagle on a carved pedestal, its wings proudly stretched to its sides, ready to fly.

Having received three awards for my performance in *House of Sand and Fog* led some people to believe that I was going to be nominated for an Oscar, too, including my husband. He and Jaleh stayed up all night waiting to hear the announcement of the nominees on TV at five-thirty in the morning.

Jaleh and Houshang had asked me if I wanted to stay up with the help of dark Persian tea to hear the result. But I told them I would rather go to sleep and act as though nothing was happening. If I was nominated, I was told a car would be waiting outside my house at 6:30 A.M. to take me to a hotel, where I would spend the rest of the day giving interviews to the media. I wanted to sound coherent and look rested in the morning. I also had no intention of letting things go to my head. What if I were not nominated?

I went to sleep early that night and was in a deep sleep when I heard Houshang whispering, "Wake up, you got it."

At first I thought I was dreaming. Then I heard all the phones in the house start ringing simultaneously, and I knew it was true. A longtime dream had come true, and I was spellbound. I was also pleased to hear that Ben Kingsley had been nominated for best actor.

I was honored and overwhelmed by the idea of opening the doors for hundreds of Middle Eastern actors who until now were bound to portray stereotypical terrorist roles most of the time.

One of the best experiences leading up to Oscar night was a delicious, unforgettable lunch with three of my favorite actresses, my fellow nominees Holly Hunter, for *Thirteen*, Marcia Gay Harden, for *Mystic River*, and Patricia Clarkson, for *Pieces of April*. Holly had kindly invited all of the supporting actress nominees, including Renée Zellweger (*Cold Mountain*) to get together a few days before the event.

Holly was staying at a nice hotel in Beverly Hills. I arrived there at one o'clock sharp and was ushered to her suite. Holly opened the door and invited me in; she was even more beautiful than in her films. Her outstanding performance in *The Piano* had already garnered her a best actress award in 1993.

Marcia Gay Harden's extraordinary performance in *Pollock* had earned her an Oscar in 2000. And Patricia had been critically acclaimed for her work, but I never had the pleasure of meeting her before our lunch at Holly's.

They all had tremendous presence, welcoming voices, and warm eyes. I was happy to see they were as friendly as I am. We spoke about films and ourselves, with our hands in the air and our theatrical voices echoing throughout the room.

Around two in the afternoon, Holly asked us if she should

go ahead and order food or wait for Renée. We all looked at each other, and I asked her if Renée had called to say she was running late. Holly said that she had never even received a response from her.

I looked at Patricia, then Marcia, and then back to Holly again and said, "Well, she could at least have called you. Don't you think?"

Holly turned red and whirled around. She called room service and dodged the obvious question to avoid further discussion concerning her rude guest.

I ONCE GAVE an interview to Radio-Sedaye-Iran in 1986 regarding my role in *Rainbow*, Kardan's play that we brought on tour to America. The host asked if I would one day consider living in L.A. and working in Hollywood. I said I wished God would hear him. He then asked me what I wished would happen to me in Hollywood, and I said I wished I would be nominated for an Oscar.

Here I was now, eighteen years later, nominated for an Academy Award. I gave interviews to prominent media people and attended magnificent galas and parties, including the Academy's famous night-before-Oscar party with my family beside me.

I got to tour couturiers and fabulous jewelry shops, received gifts, and was pampered by great beauty experts at fancy hotels, all also a part of this delightful ride.

I did not believe that I would receive that Oscar. I knew that neither the Academy nor my peers had seen my body of work and that the chance was slim. But there I sat, my heart pounding in my chest.

"And the award for best supporting actress goes to . . . Renée Zellweger!"

I was happy for her because I was just a newcomer. I could see Nicole Kidman and Catherine Zeta-Jones applauding wildly as they stood from their seats.

THE GOVERNOR'S BALL dinner party is the first place it seems everyone goes after the Oscars. We then moved to Elton John's party, followed by the prestigious *Vanity Fair* gala thrown at Morton's with Hollywood's elite. Early the next morning, I was happy to be under my covers again and fell into a sweet sleep.

The fairy tale would end and I would soon return to Earth.

40

HOLLYWOOD

I N THE FOLLOWING years, I would be working with a handful of great actors and filmmakers in more than a dozen
films and TV series, such as *Smith*, *Will and Grace*, *ER*, *Law &
Order: SVU*, *Portlandia*, and *NCIS* (with the dashing Mark
Harmon).

Working with Laura Linney in *The Exorcism of Emily Rose*
was a blast. She was witty, energetic, humble, and friendly. I
loved her acting even before I had started working with her.
But I love her even more now, having seen her at work.

In 2005, I had one of my most memorable experiences working with two of Hollywood's biggest yet humblest stars, Sandra
Bullock and Keanu Reeves, in *The Lake House*.

The movie was shot in Cook County Hospital in Chicago. It
was a huge facility and had permitted us to film in one of its
empty wings. My first scene was with Sandra Bullock. I played

Dr. Anna Klyczynski, and she played Dr. Kate Forster. In the scene, I am giving her advice about work and life.

"Take a vacation," says my character. "Get away from it all, and think what is best for you."

The two of us rehearsed the scene for the director and the camera, and I kept buttoning my white uniform during the scene. It was a bit tight at the chest, and its buttons kept popping out of place. Sandra looked at me and said, "Didn't you try on the uniform in the fitting sessions?" I said I did, back in L.A., but I figured I was portraying a doctor and not a model, so I added a few pounds to look ordinary. She laughed and said, "Aha, I know what to say to my butt next time I gain weight." She was tireless, happy, fun, and caring. We spent a lot of time talking about life and love.

Keanu was quiet, extremely polite, and a bit shy. He was always on time if not early. He never dashed in or out with his entourage after a shot, like some stars at his level do. He never left the scene, not even during the changing of the lights. He just grabbed a chair and sat close by the set with his hands crossed on his lap and his head down. It was as if he was in a body posture that insisted on privacy.

Keanu and I were in the hair-and-makeup trailer, temporarily installed under one of the famous bridges in downtown Chicago. It was six in the morning. His hairdresser mentioned how quiet the street was. He was wondering what would happen when passersby found out Keanu was in the trailer.

A half hour later we began hearing murmurs and my makeup artist took a peek out the window. He told us it seemed as if people had found out about the filming and were gathering around the trailer. I wanted to see it for myself, and looked at the crowd pointing at the trailer.

I childishly said, "Keanu, they are here for you."

Sitting calmly in his chair, he said, "No, Shohreh. They are here for cinema."

ALSO IN 2005, my agents, Peter Levin and Michael Katcher, were able to sign me up for five episodes of the popular TV show 24, starring Kiefer Sutherland. I portrayed Dina Araz, a well-rounded character with a soul: a devoted mother, a dutiful wife as well as an accessory to terrorism.

My popularity soared with viewers, and the producers brought me up to fourteen episodes that season. It was an intense show and involved a lot of twists and turns.

There was a time when the roles Middle Easterners could audition for were mostly of terrorists. As professional actors, my husband and I resisted those parts for a long time. We even gave interviews about it. We said we refused to play such roles. Our Iranian fans cheered us on. But many years had passed, and when I was offered the opportunity to play the mouthwatering, multilayered, and complex role on 24, I said, "Wait a minute," and went for it. I would not be playing a terrorist shouting, "Yallah, Yallah" ("Get moving, get moving"), which was the typical offering.

Portraying Dina Araz would also show the American audience my versatility. I intended to build my body of work for the public and for the Academy, and what better way than on prime-time TV?

Dina Araz was a sophisticated and challenging role, and I

thought I could do a good job. When I first read the script, I was fascinated by this woman's ability and courage. My decision had an artistic origin rather than a political one. I got a lot of flak for playing that role, especially from fellow Iranians, who mistakenly saw that character as a bad representation of Iranian women, or of Arabs, or of Middle Eastern women.

In fact, the character's origin was never revealed throughout the season. The audience was expected to connect the dots and draw their own conclusions about Dina and her husband Navi's motives, and this was part of the tension and suspense the show created.

I loved being a part of the cast of 24, but working with Kiefer proved challenging even for me. I can get along with almost anyone, and always have. In the end my popular character was going to become a mole as powerful as Kiefer's, which he did not like.

In one scene, Dina was going to be assassinated by a gunshot to the heart, having saved Jack Bauer's life (Kiefer's character). Dina was then to fall on her knees, her head on Jack Bauer's shoulders, who was kneeling on the floor with his arms tied behind him, look into his eyes, and say, "Save my son."

All weekend long, I practiced falling gracefully on my knees. I even bought knee pads. Houshang and Tara laughed at me and said, "Haven't you practiced enough?"

On Monday, the producers told me they were not going to kill me in front of the camera as suggested by the network. Instead the killer (the head of the terrorist cell) would order his men to take me to the other room and we would hear shots. The producers told me there was a possibility I would return to the show, but I knew in my heart that Kiefer would not agree with them for he did not want me there, period.

WHEN ON LOCATION, I love exploring the local towns, especially in exotic places such as Morocco. I was there to portray Saint Elizabeth in Catherine Hardwicke's *The Nativity Story*. I was wandering through the old bazaar in Marrakech on a Sunday afternoon when I realized I was being followed. I turned around to see a ten-year-old boy chasing me. I said, "What do you want?" He said, "Madam is artist?" in French. I was surprised and told him I was an artist, and he joyfully asked, *24*? I could not believe it. I gave him a coin and got him a sandwich and a Coke and asked him to keep the secret between us, and not to tell a soul who I was.

24 is internationally known and has a lot of fans all around the world. I am particularly popular with security guards as I go through metal detectors at airports. They always say, "The woman from *24* is here!"

Once a comedian friend of mine asked me if I was aware that I played doctors and professors most of the time. I said, "Believe me, I would love to play a maid." He replied, "Imagine you playing a maid. You would come in and say, in that deep voice of yours, 'Madam, the tea is ready.' That tea must be poisoned or there is no reason for bringing you into it."

I WISH I could play somebody's American mother. Not too long ago, I played God in the movie *The Adjustment Bureau*, but the distributor thought that a woman from a Muslim country like Iran could not appear as God in an American movie. The director, George Nolfi, who is now a good friend of mine, and the producer of the movie, Matt Damon, had no problem with it and actually thought it was quite inspired casting. But my scenes ended up somewhere between the floor and the trash can, though my name is still in the credits.

I became a working girl in Hollywood before I knew it. The industry had opened its doors to me, and the Academy nomination had brought me opportunities that would not have come any other way.

X-Men: The Last Stand was one of these opportunities. I was thrilled to play a scientist, Dr. Kavita Rao, and loved being a part of such a popular and huge film. I was stunned at how it was filmed. Great actors, movie stars, hundreds of extras, experts, and creative artists were all gathered in Canada, and with the help of highly advanced technological gadgets they took cinema to a new level. What made *X-Men* one of my great experiences in Hollywood, aside from its cast and crew, was the amount of imagination required to bring a certain truth to this genre of storytelling.

I had a scene with Kelsey Grammer, who was playing the Blue Beast. I am a fan of his TV series *Frasier* and love his voice. In fact, I wished I could talk like him, with that beautiful East Coast accent. I anxiously joined him on the set, and what did I see? An enormous Blue Beast, with a pair of big yellow eyes.

I said I had been hoping to see him in person, shake his hand and express my admiration. But his hands were covered in a pair of thick, hairy gloves, part of his costume. Instead I told him that he was the most beautiful Blue Beast ever. He wondered how many I had seen before.

Something quite bittersweet happened when we finished the film. I told the story of my departure from Iran to a colleague of mine in the movie. He asked me how my first husband could have let go of me. He was not convinced by my answer, which was that he was a painter and was inspired by Iran's beauty. He got back to me a few days later and said, "Now I know why your husband dared to leave you. He preferred Iran over you."

ANOTHER FUN AND different movie for me was *Sisterhood of the Traveling Pants 2*, based on the novels by Ann Brashares. I was not supposed to poison anyone, nor inject them with lethal serums, and I was not being stereotyped either.

I played Professor Nasrin Mehani, a simple archaeologist who teaches enthusiastic international summer students. This role would have not crossed my path had it not been for the movie's director, Sanaa Hamri. She wanted me to play the part, and I loved working with her, and the beautiful Blake Lively, whose character is a student at the camp. The movie was shot in Santorini in the Greek Island chain of the Cyclades in the Aegean Sea.

My character teaches Blake's that archaeology is not just about finding bones. "Archaeology is more than just discovering people who died. It's about learning how they lived. What made them special, or even ordinary, what they believed in and fought for, and loved."

I loved sharing a trailer with Blake and adored how her mother called her from America to make sure everything was fine. I told her how I wished I had a camera and could capture her on the phone, talking to her mom, so I could show it to those who do not think that American mothers are as vigilant as Middle Eastern ones.

Having had a tremendous time on the island with Blake, and enjoying the company of the crew and the panoramic view from my bungalow, it was time to leave. But I returned home to land one of my favorite roles of all time: Sajida, the wife of Saddam Hussein, in a coproduction between BBC Television and HBO Films, in a miniseries titled *House of Saddam*.

Many international actors, including Israeli theater and film actor Yigal Naor, who portrayed Saddam, gathered in the city of Tunis to bring to life the most intimate portrayal of a dictator's rise and fall. The writers, Alex Holmes, Stephen Butchard, and Sally El Housaini, had spent several years creating this amazing miniseries. We filmed in Tunis, Nafta, and Monastir, the three oldest cities of Tunisia. Two and a half months of intense daily work—except for the weekends and a one-week vacation after the first month—was not an easy task. But what made it tolerable was the amount of time, energy, and love that everyone, including all the good people of Tunisia, who played the hundreds of extras, put into this miniepic. I also loved filming at exotic locations, especially the scene in the Sahara.

Apparently Saddam loved camping in the Sahara with his wife and family and enjoyed hunting there with his eldest son, Uday, in the winter. It was mid-July 2008, and we were in the Sahara to re-create the scene.

Saddam's mother was played by the British actress Izabella Telezynska. We were sitting in a bohemian tent in our thick winter costumes in the middle of the Sahara with no cooling system except for our primitive straw fans. I was in a couture red wool suit worn over a wool polo. She was melting in her costume, a heavy black cloak worn head to toe, showing only her face. I was worried about her. She had a great sense of humor. She said she did not understand why we had to come to this forsaken and boiling place in the heat of the summer to portray something that originally took place in the winter. She was wondering how I kept cool and why I did not complain.

I said, "Izabella, close your eyes and imagine you are in a bath full of ice. It is cold and you are freezing. Now imagine it is so cold that you want to get out of it."

She closed her eyes and after a few minutes of struggling with reality she said, "It isn't working, Shohreh." We both laughed.

Izabella and I explored historical sites, went to museums, and shopped at the old bazaars every chance we got. I will never forget the day she left. All the actors stayed at a five-star resort hotel next to the beach outside the city of Tunis for almost two months. It had become home to us. The manager of the hotel, Mr. Shokri, knew us by our names and did his best to accommodate us.

It was six-thirty in the morning on a Saturday when the ear-piercing emergency sirens went off. I jumped out of bed, went to my door, and knew we did not have much time if it was a bomb alert. I opened the door to see a half-naked man peeking down the hallway from his door in a room facing mine.

I grabbed my robe and ran for my life. I noticed there were only three of us running: a young Israeli couple holding their baby and me.

We took the stairs to the lobby only to find out that it was just a false alarm. All the Arabs, Europeans, and other clientele seemed to have had no problem with the alarm. I was standing there in my robe, embarrassed. But the young couple was so grateful to God for saving their child that they could not care less about standing in their nightgowns. Mr. Shokri apologized for the inconvenience and invited the three of us to breakfast.

Akbar Kurtha, who played Saddam's trusted secretary Kamel Hana, also spent a lot of time with Izabella, because she reminded him of his own mother. Seeing her off, Akbar asked Izabella if she had anything to do with the alarm, and whether she did it to avoid paying her bill. She was still laughing in the car that took her to the airport. I was sad to see her go as the dust rose in her wake.

41

ACCOLADES

Two and a half months of intense work paid off. I received the prestigious Emmy Award in 2009 for best supporting actress, for portraying Saddam's wife.

I had asked my husband and my daughter to look me in the eye and tell me if my name was announced. I have this fear of making a mistake and thinking my name is called when it is not. So when Kevin Bacon and his wife, Kyra Sedgwick, pronounced my name correctly, I was still not quite sure if it was me. I looked at my daughter and she nodded, then I looked at my husband and he gave me a look that could easily be read as: *What on earth are you waiting for?*

I gathered all my energy, got up, and walked toward the stage, my head down, still wondering if it was my name that they had called out.

Then it dawned on me that I was not on my own, that I was

representing millions of Middle Easterners, including Iranian women who most probably were watching me via the Internet or on various Middle Eastern TV programs aired on satellites. Along with the million-dollar earrings and bracelet loaned from Boucheron, I wore a green plastic band on my wrist representing the progressive Green Movement back home in Iran. I waved my arm proudly. I was there on their behalf. I took a deep breath gently, held my long skirt up a tad to avoid any kind of embarrassing falls, and began walking up the stairs with my head held high.

I thanked all the good people who had helped me receive the award. I was choked up with emotion as well, trying hard not to shed a tear as I received the award, given to me by my peers, for my role in *House of Saddam*.

RIGHT AFTER *House of Saddam*, Cyrus Nowrasteh called me about his screenplay, adapted from a French-Iranian journalist's book *The Stoning of Soraya M*, based on a true story.

Sahebjam, portrayed by Jim Caviezel (*The Passion of the Christ*), visits Iran after the revolution and is trapped in a remote Iranian village when his car breaks down. He is approached by a woman—my character, Zahra—who tells him the horrifying story of her niece being stoned to death. The two sit down together while his car is being repaired at the only body shop in the village. He records the conversation with his tape recorder. He must now escape with the story, risking his life to share it with the world.

I had been desperately waiting for someone to bring this barbaric act of punishment to light in the Western world. After reading the screenplay, I let Cyrus know that I would do any-

thing for it to be made and was wondering if he knew any producers who would be willing to risk their money on it. Clearly
this was not a commercial film, and not many executives are
fond of humanitarian subjects.

He told me that Stephen McEveety and John Shepherd, the
founders of the production company M Power, were up to produce the film. I was thrilled knowing it would happen. Steve
would not shy away from the material; he was one of the producers of *The Passion of the Christ*.

The movie was shot in Jordan. All the exteriors, including
the stoning scene, were filmed in a village called Dana in one
month. The rest of the film was shot in Amman, the capital of
Jordan, on seven hills in a circle around the center of the town,
forming a 360-degree view of this ancient city.

A dedicated cast and crew, along with the good people of the
village of Dana, brought to life the horrifying story of man's
brutality in a typically misogynistic society.

Everything about this film was a miracle, including its release. It was not only made in under a year, but it also coinci-
dentally premiered at the time when the Iranian Green
Movement began a series of protests following the fraudulent
election of Mahmoud Ahmadinejad. Millions of young Iranians
poured out into the streets wearing green tops or headbands or
scarves protesting against the regime and demanding Ahmadinejad's removal from office in 2009.

The movie did what it was supposed to do. It not only en-
lightened its audience outside Iran but was also an eye-opener
to the people who thought that stoning was ancient history. It
garnered great reviews and was well received by its audience.

Regretfully, the Green Movement in Iran was defeated and

many of the young protesters who marched peacefully on the streets were tortured or killed. Among them was Neda, a young woman who was shot in the neck and died on the street. Someone with a cell phone camera caught images of this tragedy, which then horrified the world.

42

TOMORROW AND YESTERDAY

MAHMOUD AHMADINEJAD CAME to power in Iran through a fraudulent election. His second term will expire in 2013. Although the Green Movement, which had asked for a fair election, has gone underground now, it is my hope that they will advance their cause in 2013 and that the blood of young people like Neda would not have been shed in vain.

Slowly but surely, the people of the Middle East are losing their fear and gaining their freedom. Thousands of Tunisians, Egyptians, Yemenis, Syrians, and others are marching, striving to build nations where no citizen is jailed, beaten, or killed because they speak the truths within their minds and hearts. They seek jobs, housing, and wages that allow proud men and women to provide for their families. They are demanding the liberty to elect governments that for the first time ever will speak in their name.

I have watched the images of people in Tunis, Cairo, and Sana'a with a mixture of elation, hope, foreboding, and, yes, fear. And I pray that in the places located beyond the reach of television people do not lose their voice to fear, but rather find the call for democracy. For Americans, free speech and free pursuit of happiness are easy and expected, but for nearly everyone living in the Middle East, they are neither.

I was born in Iran, and I lived there as a young woman during the 1979 revolution. Thirty-four years later, I have seen many moments in which history has indeed repeated itself. Back in 1979, Iranians of every background lost their fear and found their voices. Together, they marched in the streets, as neither the Shah nor his secret police could silence their piercing, full-throated demands for freedom, democracy, and fundamental respect. The Shah was overthrown, only to be replaced by the Islamic Republic that today persecutes and imprisons any citizen who questions its politics. Those who fought for Iran's liberation thought that nothing could be worse than the Shah. Unfortunately they were wrong.

May the fate that has befallen Iran never place its hands upon the freedom struggles taking place now throughout the region.

Finally, fitfully and fearfully, many of the region's autocrats are hearing the voices of their people. But will they listen to their message? To the world, the message from my Middle Eastern brethren is loud and clear: no more oppression, no more dictatorship, and no more hopelessness. This new generation of liberators is marching bravely for the right to choose their fate.

Thomas Jefferson wrote, "When people fear their government, there is tyranny; when government fears the people, there is liberty."

This is what I wish for my birth country, Iran.

May once again the younger generation of Iran pass through the love alleys in the springtime, hand in hand, and recite poetry to each other beneath the heaving yellow jasmines on the walls, in a free society.

WHILE FINISHING THIS book, I am in the midst of a family reunion in Calabasas. My mother has come to stay with me for a couple of months, as my father passed away six years ago from a stroke. My brothers are all here with me. Shahram has come in from London, where he now is involved in the field of social work. Shahriar has made his way from Istanbul to San Diego, where he now sells pharmaceutical products. And Sean— formerly Shahrokh—lives in Hawaii as an I.T. engineer for one of Donald Trump's hotels. My daughter, Tara-Jane, is currently a graduate student studying film at Chapman University. A free spirit, she also has a band, and like Houshang and I once did, she tours around the United States with her band called Aerial Stereo. Houshang is busy being creative and writing new plays. At night we stay up until 3:00 a.m. reminiscing, laughing, and crying about yesterday, when we were young.

My brothers and I purchased live silkworms or caterpillars, ten or twenty at a time, from the markets when we were kids, and placed them in a shoe box on a bed of thoroughly washed green leaves from our neighbor's mulberry tree that had generously laid its branches on our roof. We then kept replacing the dried, toothed leaves with fresh ones while the silkworms were weaving and creating colorful cocoons with their saliva, just like a cobweb. Some people think silk is made from the silk-worm, though it is actually made from the cocoons of a silk moth. Their growth process was like that of a butterfly. We watched their metamorphoses in awe as the silk moths or white butterflies emerged, leaving their colorful cocoons behind for us to collect.

ACKNOWLEDGMENTS

FIRST AND FOREMOST I would like to thank my friend and manager, Tamara Houston, who encouraged me to take my bits and pieces of writings seriously, and to write my memoir.

I would also like to thank my editor, Claire Wachtel, for her patience and advice, and all the members of my great team at HarperCollins for their enthusiasm, support, and love.

Many thanks to all of my friends who have patiently waited a year and a half for me to finish writing this book so we can party again.

Thanks, too, to all of my fellow Iranians for their unflagging support of my work.

I am also so grateful to my mother and my brothers for standing by me in pursuing my dreams, including in writing this book.

My father, Anushiravan Vaziritabar, passed away in 2006. We saw each other only a handful of times in the thirty years since the Iranian revolution in 1979, when I left behind my beloved family; my dog, Pasha; my colleagues and friends; and my birth country, Iran, in pursuit of freedom and democracy. I could not even visit him at his deathbed for fear of losing my life over my beliefs. Instead, I spent hours on the phone with my mother at his side, to listen to his last weakening breaths.

The news of my father's death came early in the morning when I was about to shoot a scene for a new television drama. I was in a state of denial at first and turned my back to the bearer of the bad news. I had lost a noble man whose unconditional love, wisdom, and guidance had brought me here.

My mind filled with images of my father; they flew before my eyes just like shooting stars. I was picturing him with my three brothers and me, helping us with our homework and the multiplication table after school, playing backgammon and solving puzzles with us on the weekends. He took us to hospitals twice a year, and had us share our donations of sweets and fruits with the disadvantaged patients who had no visitors. It was his way of teaching us.

I specifically remember the day he taught me how to waltz to "The Blue Danube." I was sixteen years old and proud to watch my parents dancing a waltz or tango so effortlessly and in total harmony at our family parties and weddings. One two three, one two three, says my father. I am taking the steps back and forth, holding onto my father's arms, spinning around, occasionally stepping on my father's toes. He is looking at me with pride and joy.

I spent the rest of that day mourning his loss in silence, feeling proud of being so lucky to have him in my life and to have him with me now and forever.

ABOUT THE AUTHOR

SHOHREH AGHDASHLOO WON the Emmy Award for Outstanding Supporting Actress for HBO's *House of Saddam* and was the first Iranian actress to be nominated for an Academy Award for her role in *House of Sand and Fog*. She has starred in the Fox series *24*, and has been featured in a number of television shows and films. Born and raised in Tehran, she now lives in Los Angeles.